Prince Edward Island Tales

SECOND EDITION

Poems and Stories written by members of the Montague Library Writers Guild

i

Wood Island Prints
670 Trans-Canada Highway, RR 1
Belle River, PE C0A 1B0
(902) 962-3335 schultz@pei.sympatico.ca

For information about the Writers Guild you may contact:
Swarna Chandrasekera, Librarian
Montague Public Library
Montague, PE C0A 1R0
(902) 838-2928 montague.gov.pe.ca

Printing and binding by:
Lightning Source Inc. (US)
1246 Heil Quaker Blvd.
La Vergne, TN 37086 USA
Voice: (615 213-5815
Fax: (615) 213-4725
Email: inquiry@lightningsource.com
www.lightningsource.com

ISBN 978-0-9783995-6-6

Cover photo *Graham's Pond* by Tom Rath

Introduction

Whether we're sitting in a booth at Tim Horton's, blocking the aisles at Atlantic Superstore, or catching our breath on a bench along the Confederation Trail, we're bound to be chatting about the Island, or other Islanders.

It's just a fact of life here on Prince Edward Island. We tell stories, we share gossip, and we talk about the Island itself—today's weather, our garden, the latest "issue," employment, politics, and then tomorrow's weather.

This book shares what some Islanders currently living in Eastern Prince Edward Island think, talk, and write about.

A sense of pride runs through many of our stories and verses. We like our home, and given the opportunity, we'll show it off to you like someone who has just finished redecorating their living room.

Other stories are not so pleasant. Some reflect the very real challenges we as Islanders face as residents of a small part of Canada with more than its share of hard times.

As you drive around the Island, you may pass by old houses abandoned by the families they once sheltered. Similarly, when you look into the weathered complexion of fishers and farmers, you might catch the grim look of someone who is struggling to keep afloat financially. We overcome many challenges, usually. We survive.

Some of us qualify in what is called the Classic definition of an *Islander*—we were born here. Quite possibly we live in the same house that sheltered our parents, grandparents, and earlier forebears, too.

Others of us *Come From Away (CFA)* or, as we prefer to say, we are *Islanders by Choice (IBC)* or *Islanders on Purpose (IOP)*. We may have been born elsewhere, but have now adopted Prince Edward Island as our home.

We all share a passion for our Province.

This book stems from our participation in the Montague Library Writers Guild, a gathering of area residents who enjoy recording on paper (or computer screen) our experiences and memories. We meet at the Library and read to each other, and discuss our writings and the themes they present.

Are we special? You could say that—special in the same sense as any group of individuals who share a common interest in writing, such as we do.

That common interest leads us to talking to you, the reader, about how we see life here in Eastern Prince Edward Island. Some of the 50 stories you find between these pages detail our own life experiences, some are triggered by those chats with other Islanders, and some are fabrications, pieces of fiction.

If you take the opportunity to attend an evening *ceilidh* in some Community Hall, enjoying performances of singers, dancers and fiddlers, you may also hear a reading by one of the authors whose works are between the covers of this book.

In any case, thanks to the enthusiastic support of Montague Librarian Swarna Chandrasekera, you now can read these stories and verses at your own pace, and in a comfortable chair in your own home.

Special thanks to Hugh MacDonald, an award-winning poet, writer, editor and neighbour, who accepted our invitation to share one of his works in this collection. Thanks also to Jill Schultz and Prof. Milton for proofreading the finished book.

Enjoy!

Tom Rath, Editor/Project Coordinator

Foreword

The members of the Montague Library Writers Guild are proud to present the second edition of their collected works, *Prince Edward Island Tales*. This edition differs slightly from the first edition in that two authors withdrew their work and the remaining authors contributed additional stories and poems. Members of the guild meet monthly at the Montague Library. We share, discuss, and critique our writings with the goal of encouraging each other and sharpening the quality of our work. Visitors are always welcome and there are no fees to become a Guild member.

The Guild has expanded its activity to include public readings and sharing of the writing process. We have entertained audiences at Perrin's Villa, Montague *Summerfest*, Wood Islands *Ferry Festival*, the Arts Center, and Montague High School.

Many people have contributed to the making of this book. We would like to thank our editor/project coordinator, Tom Rath, and our publisher, Tom Schultz, for their time and dedication in getting this book to print. Also a special thanks to Montague Librarian Swarna Chandrasekera for her continual encouragement and support.

We hope you will enjoy this book as much as we have had the pleasure of communicating the collective spirit of the community through our writings about beautiful Prince Edward Island.

Joanne Collicott McGuigan, President
Montague Library Writers Guild

Panmure Island

Joanne Collicott McGuigan

Joanne Collicott McGuigan lives with her husband, Wayne, and their cat, Angel, a few kilometres south of Montague, P.E.I. Joanne considers herself, not *from away*, but an *Islander by marriage*. Her husband's ancestors, Jack "Jock" McGuigan and wife Peggy Hughes, emigrated from Co. Monaghan, Ireland and arrived in Prince Edward Island around 1840. They settled in the St. Mary's Road area.

Since meeting in Oshawa, Ontario, Joanne and Wayne spent every summer on the Island, and now they live here permanently. Joanne feels it is exactly like Lucy Maude Montgomery, author of *Anne of Green Gables*, said, "Once you come to the Island you feel you have come home."

The oldest of five children, Joanne spend her childhood in the province of New Brunswick. In the spring of 1997, New Brunswick was connected to P.E.I. by the Confederation Bridge. The bridge is a distance of 12.9 kilometres and the longest bridge over ice-covered waters.

Joanne enjoys walking in the fresh air and listening to Celtic music, such as played here in the Maritimes. The secrets of the mind, the universe and the betterment of mankind have always been important interests to her.

Joanne's parents met during the 2nd World War in England where her mother was a nurse. Her mother was from Co. Mayo, Ireland and her father a Canadian soldier from Canterbury, New Brunswick.

Although working in the banking field in Oshawa, Ontario,

was Joanne's primary profession, for a time she also wrote a dream analysis column for a local paper. Another article by Joanne is a story about her mother, Catherine Collicott, being a War Bride. It is available to read at Canada's Immigration Museum, Pier 21, Halifax, Nova Scotia.

Other books by the author available at amazon.com are: *Child of Danaan*, a story about the loss of Joanne's son and *The Dream Mechanism*, a compilation of the dream analysis column..

Confederation Bridge--Main Gateway to PEI

Prince Edward Island Hospitality

In our busy, busy lives do we still take the time to greet our neighbours, stop to help a stranger in trouble or take just a minute to smile as we walk past an unknown person?

Growing up in a small village, it was customary to greet everyone you met on the street with a smile and, "Hello" or, "How are you?" When I went to an Ontario city in my late teens, there were a lot of funny glances as I still greeted everyone with a smile and hello. I thought this tradition of greeting another human being was just good manners.

There is a need in our society for mothers to tell their children not to talk to strangers, but a simple "Hello" can make the difference between a good day and a not-so-good day to many people. The conversation doesn't have to go any further than a simple greeting.

Of course hospitality goes deeper than that. It also includes acts of providing service and kindness to whomever is in need, whether friend or stranger.

Along with good manners, food is an important ingredient in hospitality. For example, a cake, supper dish or other delicacy is often brought to the home of a new neighbour as a way of introduction. Such is the case here in Prince Edward Island.

When a death or serious illness occurs, the neighbours, friends and church members generally bring food to the family to show their support to the grieving family. Cards of Thanks in the local newspapers, such as I have often seen in the Eastern Graphic, will often mention, along with other things, sincere gratitude to all who brought food to the home of grieving families.

The hospitality of Prince Edward Island is well known. The expression, 'Would you care for a spot of tea?" still rings true. If a friend or stranger happens by at dinner time, there will swiftly be another place set at the table.

Many times I have spoken with an elderly gentleman, Steward MacKenna. He is often seen walking around the Town of Montague. Steward is eight-seven years old but still is able to get around with the help of his cane. He has the keen mind and sharp piercing eyes of a much younger man.

One afternoon I sat down beside him on the bench in the local grocery store. We talked about P.E.I. and how things were in his younger days. He told me stories about when he was the grave-digger in this area and how he used to pick up my husband's maternal grandfather and give him a ride to funerals, usually the ones held at

St. Paul's Church

St. Paul's Church in Sturgeon. If my husband's grandfather was living today, he would be well over one hundred years old. I thanked Steward for being kind to him.

"Well," he said with a puzzled look, as if I should know it was always part of his life to help other people, "Hughie and Katie Mc-Dougall were wonderful people, and I felt it was a great honour to know them."

I mentioned to Steward I wanted to write an article on the hospitality of the Island. He gave a little grin and said the people here have always opened their hearts to anyone in need.

Steward then proceeded to tell me of the time in his younger days when he was helping a neighbour with the haying and suddenly a stranger came into the field. The ragged dress of the stranger and his gaunt expression were of someone who hadn't eaten in days. In those hard times, it was common for hobos, or tramps (as they were often called), to knock on your door and ask if you might have a crust of bread or something for them to eat. It was around noon and the men were getting ready to go into the house for lunch. The neighbour invited the stranger to come in with the rest of the haying crew and share their meal.

When the neighbour's wife heard there was another mouth to feed at the table she threw up her hands and said to her husband, "It is mighty strange that you would invite a complete stranger to eat with us!" He replied, "It would be mighty strange if I didn't!"

And there you have it—the secret of hospitality at its finest.

A Little Spot of the Potcheen

My husband found copper pipe and a rusted metal jug in the woods on our property here on Prince Edward Island. He thought it was remnants of an old still. It is a well known fact that at one time a number of stills were set up on the Island to produce a powerful home-made brew referred to as moonshine or white lightning. To escape being detected by the law, the stills were usually hidden away from prying eyes.

Path to the Still

Anyone swaggering home after an afternoon of testing out the powerful distilled liquid could cause an argument in the household. The stills were hurriedly dismantled if word got out that an angry wife threatened to report this illegal activity to the authorities.

As many Islanders have roots going back to Ireland, this tradition of making your own liquor seems to carry back to the old country. *Potcheen* is Irish moonshine produced typically from potatoes but can also be made from grain.

I had occasion to sample this potent alcohol a few years before my mother passed away. My sister Rose and I travelled with her to the family home in Co. Mayo, situated in the West of Ireland.

One Sunday morning, after attending Mass, we went to visit Agnes, a first cousin of my mother who lived with her husband Tom on the outskirts of Ballina.

After my mother and Agnes had their tearful reunion greeting, Agnes's big and burly red-haired husband brought out a tray containing a bottle of Paddy's Irish whiskey along with a bottle of the homemade potcheen.

He said to my mother, "Now, would you being having a little spot of the potcheen, Kathleen?" Mother knowingly smiled and said she would be just as happy with a cup of Agnes' fine tea. Wanting to try everything pertaining to our Irish heritage, Rose and I said we would have a little spot of the potcheen.

I took a large mouthful from the exceptionally large glass handed to me. The powerful liquid burned my throat all the way down to the lower parts of my anatomy. Trying to act normal and still breathing fire, I set the glass down on a small table beside me. Rose was not so easily discouraged from the deadly concoction. She emptied her glass in record time and didn't seem to suffer any ill effects.

The two of us smiled and listened as Mother and Agnes talked about their childhood and of leaving food out in the meadow for the little fairy people. From their conversation, I gleaned the leprechauns were part of this fairy group; except for their diminutive size, they seemed the most like humans.

Agnes said, "This wonderful magical fairy group lived in the otherworld dimension called *Tir na nOg*, the land where you never grow old."

Mother added, "There were secret portals or openings from this land of youth where the fairies or little people could come into our world. Most of the time they were invisible but sometimes they would appear to humans. It was thought their magical powers could be used for good or mischief."

She went on and explained that some of the Leprechauns were shoemakers. It was thought the gentle tapping of their hammers would sometimes be heard in the distance. Others were merrymakers; they danced and played their music in the meadows.

"Upon hearing the tic, tic, tic of the tiny hammer, blow of the hornpipe or squeal of the fiddle, food and drink would be left in the field or area where the faint tapping or soft musical notes were heard."

Tom, his face now almost as red as his hair, stood up and said, "The leprechauns were not adverse to a drop or two of the potcheen being left for them. It was wise to keep them in good humour as they were known for playing pranks on humans. I declare, if it's good enough for the leprechauns, it's good enough for anyone."

Agnes and Mother both admitted to occasionally leaving a glass of potcheen in the field hoping the leprechauns would drink it and make some of their dreams come true. Magically the glass would be empty the next day.

As they laughed and reminisced about the potcheen and the little people, I realized Rose had become very quiet and her face was getting redder by the minute. For someone not accustomed to drink, one glass had rendered my sister almost paralyzed.

My mother and I somehow managed to get Rose back to our room where she slept it off the rest of the day! From that afternoon onward we vowed to leave the drinking of the potcheen to the little people.

My conclusion from the little spot of potcheen I tasted in Ballina? "If the stills of Prince Edward Island have produced alcohol as strong as the potcheen I tasted in Ireland, it may be best to leave it in the fields and meadows for the leprechauns!"

Old Bob and Jane

Old Bob and Jane; a peculiar pair;
Locked in a union with no love to share.
At the first blush of marriage, all was quite well,
But thanks to hard years, her warmth for him fell.
Raising three children had taken its toll;
Marriage weighed heavy on her fragile soul.
Old Bob was helpless to lighten Jane's load.
To her, a once-prince had turned into a toad.

Arguments, slights, and a simmering fight—
Jane decided Old Bob wasn't really that bright.
The mere thought of mending for him was the pits;
He braved bitter cold with holes in his mitts.
Her temper was legend; in our small village it was said,
"Since middle-age, she'd quite lost her head."
A scrappy wife now, with the tongue of a viper;
Whose husband was only to jig to her piper.

Jane banished Old Bob from their marriage bed,
From then on, he slept in a cold rundown shed.
Still chopping and lugging in fresh firewood;
Old Bob kept her house warm as he could.
The fire of her love had long since gone out,
Could never revive—cold ashes, no doubt.
Old Bob and Jane have both passed away.
I wish I had better memories of them today.

Waiting Impatiently

Every morning before light of dawn,
Before the birds begin their song
Two cats decide I should arise.
They jump upon my rumpled bed
And make half-circles 'round my head.

If these first efforts seem in vain;
Another way drives me insane.
It's just five-thirty on the clock.
The old cat glares up from the floor;
The young one meows loudly by the door.

I shake the sleep from mind and eyes,
Then stagger out to give their prize.
Triumphant cats; one on each side,
My every move watched on the way
As we begin another day.

CC and Angel (Waiting)

Coyote Stick

When Hubby says," Let's go for a walk through the old forest," I always reply, "Wait until I get my coyote stick to take with me."

The coyote stick is just an ordinary walking stick I made out of the wood from a pin cherry tree. I have peeled some of the red speckled bark away from the handle and applied a few coats of varnish to make it nice and smooth. I always take it with me when I walk the path through the old forest.

Like most Islanders, I am concerned with keeping our beautiful Isle green and clean. I share their ideals about recycling, preserving the natural environment, and keeping the drinking water and streams free from pesticides and contaminants. I believe we need to protect all the animals who also share our land. Being an animal lover, I normally found this philosophy an easy one to follow until the disappearance of the rabbits and cats in my area.

Prince Edward Island does not have the large wildlife, such as deer, bear and moose, common in the other Maritime Provinces. However, in the spring, I was pleased to see some of our native, smaller animals coming around the property. Rabbits have been scarce the last few years and, then, out of nowhere, a black rabbit appeared. For months the black rabbit could be seen coming onto the lawn in the early morning and late evening to nibble on the clovers and dandelions. Since wild rabbits are not normally black, he must have been a domestic rabbit that had escaped his cage or someone had grown tired of him and released him into the wild to fend for himself. He would be an easier prey than a wild rabbit as his fur did not change colour. The changing of the fur colour to match the seasons of the year is a natural camouflage for a wild rabbit.

Besides the black rabbit, there often could be seen an adult wild rabbit and a baby rabbit munching on the grass and leafy weeds along the edge of the lawn. Rabbits are known to live in groups, but the two wild brown rabbits never socialized with the

black rabbit. Perhaps it was a natural precaution: he was ostra-
cized because of the black colour of his fur.

Since the black rabbit was always grazing alone, Hubby and
I decided to call him Orbison. This was after the late singer, Roy
Orbison, who was famous for the song, *Only the Lonely*. Orbison
was quite tame as I could walk within a few feet of him before he
hopped off into the woods. In comparison, the two wild rabbits
seemed alert at all times and quickly vanished as soon as they
saw me.

Then there were the raccoon and the skunk who liked to
tear clumps of dirt out of the lawn. This was to find and consume
the white juicy grubs they would hear moving under the grass
roots. The raccoon was terribly overweight as each evening he
would feast on the food the neighbours left outside for stray cats.
Although the closest neighbour lived a fair distance away, the
raccoon would still make his nightly rounds to see what food he
could scavenge. Then he would swagger over to use our lawn as
his private toilet. Much to his chagrin, Hubby would have to
scoop the raccoon feces from the lawn just about every day. One
evening I saw the raccoon outside the back door and I hollered at
him to go away. The cantankerous, chubby critter glared up at
me, then climbed the nearby apple tree and started shaking a
branch. He then climbed down and scampered off into the old for-
est without even eating any of the apples he shook off the tree.
Nevertheless, the apples did not go to waste as the next evening
a family of five grouse came by to peck at them. Other birds and
the chipmunks also loved to eat the apples. Together with what I
used to make pies, nothing on that apple tree ever went to waste.

All these animals
were fine and dandy to
have around but there was
another animal slinking
around in the old forest
that I was a bit worried
about. The hair would
stand up on the back of my
neck when I heard howling

at night. Sometimes while walking in the old forest I would catch a whiff of mangy fur and know a coyote was nearby.

The old forest has its own unique appeal where the bustling clatter of the modern world is blocked by the peaceful invisible guardians of nature. Besides the rustling noise of my own movements, the only sound is the occasional chattering of a chipmunk or the fluttering of a bird's wing. At times the silence of the woods is broken by a squeak caused by the swaying of an ancient spruce or poplar tree. Some are so old they have already fallen to the ground or their fall has been caught by the branches of younger, stronger trees.

When asked by a friend why I needed to carry my coyote stick when I walked through the old forest, I replied, "Because there are coyotes nearby and I need the stick to defend myself if one decides to attack."

The standard retort was that coyotes do not attack humans and they are more afraid of you than vice versa.

"That is all well and good," I would say, "but they have big teeth and wild dogs might be running with them."

I have seen coyotes on three occasion—not in the old forest but near the house. My first sighting was a mother coyote and her three pups. This was a few years ago when Hubby and I were only able to come to the Island for the summer. Mother coyote looked like a smaller version of a Collie dog. From the upstairs window I saw her at the edge of the lawn, slightly hidden in the tree line, as she watched her pups come and play near the front door. Perhaps they had been getting food from other people and she thought I would put some out. The pups were so cute that I wanted to feed them but thought better of having them stay around. Another time I pulled in the driveway and the car headlights picked out an adult coyote circling the house. At that time I had two cats I was trying to keep inside. I think the coyote knew they were in the house and was hungrily waiting for them to come outside. The last time I saw a coyote was a year ago. It was early in the morning when it sauntered out of the old forest behind the house. The coyote hesitated briefly by the elephant plants on the north side of the house and then nonchalantly loped across the road. Perhaps it was going back to the den to sleep the daylight hours away after a night of foraging for food.

By this October, Orbison, the black rabbit, had disappeared. Also missing were the mother rabbit and her baby. One of my cats, C.C., had resented all my attempts to keep him housebound. I finally relented and let him go outside and he was also a casualty. There was never any evidence of what may have happened to these animals, but the coyotes were still howling at night and the mischievous raccoon and the grub-digging skunk were still making their rounds every evening.

For a week after C.C.'s disappearance I called for him every evening before retiring for the night. In case he came back after I was asleep and cried to come in the house, I left the bedroom window slightly open. I phoned the vet clinic and was told the great horned owl might have taken him but they had a report of other cats missing in nearby areas and coyotes were suspected of being the perpetrators.

Coyotes must also be fed and will eat whatever is smaller on the food chain, be it, foxes, rabbits, mice or other rodents. Their typical diet would be small mammals, insects, reptiles and sometimes fruit. When rabbits are scarce, then the cats are in more danger of being their next meal. There is a story about the coyotes being cunning enough to slip through an electric fence and bring down sheep just a few miles from where I live. Most would agree something must be done about an animal when it is preying on livestock. I would never advocate the extermination of all coyotes as they are not, on a whole, harmful because most of their diet is made up of destructive rodents. This is part of the natural balance of nature.

U.S. President, Teddy Roosevelt, in 1901, was famous for quoting the West African proverb when dealing with political issues, "Speak softly and carry a big stick."

Here in Canada and in keeping with my philosophy to treat all animals humanly, I will be walking softly and carrying my coyote stick through the old forest as long as there are coyote sightings on Prince Edward Island.

Sobeys Liar's Bench
Steward McKenna & Roy Penny

The Liar's Bench At the Grocery Store

The old gentleman peered intensely across the way
As I gathered my groceries on this fair Island day.
Soon on the Liar's Bench another man sat
I could tell by the nod they had often met.
While some come and sit and wait for the wife,
Others make it a part of their everyday life.
Each could recall the taste of the briny sea,
When the cold and the damp leaves its mark on thee;
Where they sailed, caught lobster, and fished.
Cruise those waters again? They oftentimes wished
On the Liar's Bench at the grocery store.

Stories of lost loves and hard times gone by
So sad they would bring a tear to the eye.
Of haying and horses, their habits and traits;
Of good-looking women each had taken on dates.
Of Seamus who's come home from the West,
Of loved ones who have now gone to their rest.
Tales of life and death unfolds the door
With eulogies to comrades gone before;
Joking, the pale rider did not come last night
Seeing land and sea in comical second sight
On the Liar's Bench at the grocery store.

Even my mate is waiting for me today
Was the talk fact or fiction-he'll never say;
Of the government, the potatoes, the weather to dread
Of tilling and milking and whose life hangs by a thread.
Picking up my groceries and passing their way,
"Good afternoon," I always smile to them each day.
So if you have a few minutes to spare
Think up some gossip and park yourself there.
Why even a woman is welcome to share
News with Steward and Kenny, Wayne and Blair
On the Liar's Bench at the grocery store.

Why? Why? Why?

You will get no answer from me
On why we are born; on why we must die,
Or why in a dark, lonely grave we will lie.
I'll just leave the answer to thee.
But I'll oft think of Mary, felled by a stroke,
Her short night of dreams; long days without hope.
A teacher by trade and so smart to boot
She was pledged to be wife to a handsome young brute.
Why, why, why!

On the unpaved road leading up to her school
She wore modest dress; a style that she chose
Perhaps long dark coat, sensible saddle shoes.
Neatly groomed always. No high-fashion tools.
Then one day, like lightning, the word spread around
A stroke had brought this young woman down.
Mary was stricken while all on her own.
The only words now she could quietly drone,
"Why, why, why?"

Mary walked slowly, that same gravel road
One side rendered useless by the stroke.
To avoid bruising the tip of her motionless toe,
She'd throw out the limp leg each step, to and fro.
With a cane to support her paralyzed side
And a sadness seen deep in her blue eyes
The dream of a wedding had suddenly died.
What was left for this woman who now only cried,
"Why, why, why?"

Whenever we talk of our earthly existence,
"What is our purpose? To whom bear we witness?"
I think of young Mary and all she held dear.
For after her stroke, it was so very clear
She thought she had nothing left for her lover.
Mary went home to live with her lonely old Mother.
And many a question was now hers to ponder.
With nary an answer; she was just left to wonder
Why, why, why?

Gary Gray

Gary's family came to Prince Edward Island from Scotland by way of Nova Scotia. He was born and raised near Coleman, P.E.I. In 2002 Gary suffered a massive stroke and has battled his way to what he now warmly refers to as his *new normal*. He's adjusted his life in order to recover many of the abilities he lost and is working hard to help others who are stroke survivors find their new normal too.

Gary has written articles about his own stroke experience and recently wrote a four page information piece on the need for an Acute Care Stroke Unit in Prince Edward Island. He joined the Montague Library Writers' Guild to stimulate his mind. Since joining he has been inspired to write memoirs of his early years as a native Islander as well as continuing with his articles about stroke recovery, evolving internet-based technology, and healthy ways to incorporate physical exercises into everyday life. Gary's work can be found on the web by visiting his website at http://www.81x.com/garydotgray/home. You will find the links to his blogs there.

When he isn't writing, Gary enjoys taking in the island's beauty on his daily walks and meeting friends for tea; most of all he is glad he is once again able to enjoy the relaxed lifestyle Prince Edward Island is famous for.

A Beautiful Day To Be Born

The principal actor was my mother, Belle, who lay in a double steel rail bed in the north bedroom of our house. Mom was about to deliver her third child when the doctor was called away on an emergency. This left only her mother, Annie, to assist with the birth. Annie was no stranger to delivering babies as she had served the people of the nearby Fortune Cove community for many years as a midwife and nurse in time of need. Gram Annie had lost her second baby in childbirth and been left with a permanent back injury but this hadn't stopped her from helping others who needed her.

My father Dave had been dispatched with his horse and wagon in search of a doctor to deliver the baby. He returned with Dr. George in tow. Pup Lawson, my grandfather, had left for his Mill Road farm to hitch up the team to the old plough and go a couple of rounds in the field (just to be

Going a Couple of Rounds

able to say that he had ploughed a field on December the 4th). Where my brother Lawson was, no one knew. It was hard to keep track of ten-year-old boys in those days. My sister Irene was twelve and hung as close as possible to her best friend Ruby who was a much older and wiser sixteen. They awaited with much anticipation the arrival of the new sister or brother.

Without a great deal of fanfare the brand new baby boy arrived about mid-morning. Dr. George had walked in just in time to congratulate my mother on the successful delivery of a healthy baby boy. He never disclosed my length and weight but did take the time to stroll over to the bedroom window and proclaim, "What a beautiful day to be born on!"

My mother and father had collaborated over the past months on names like Willard and David and Gordon, but in the case of a boy, they had finally agreed upon (drum roll please)...*Gary David Gray*. I was a healthy baby and received the best of care from my mother, grandmother and sister. But something was just not right. I wanted to sleep more than what was thought normal, and I refused to nurse. So Mom bundled me up and with my Dad took me to see Mrs. Turner, the health nurse in O'Leary. After an examination by the nurse, Dr. George appeared and proceeded to probe my rectum with his finger and wipe it on my clean blanket. (My mom was not impressed!) He then proclaimed, "He appears healthy and I just don't know what the problem is." The nurse took my mom to one side and said, "He is a lazy baby and would sooner sleep than eat. Wash his face with a cold damp cloth to keep him awake and make him eat at regular times." So my mom and dad took me home and set about following the instructions as the nurse had laid them out. In time their efforts proved successful and I began to eat and grow like any other healthy baby.

My mom remained grateful to that nurse for the remainder of her days. She would say often, "Without her telling us what to do we would not have known, and the baby would not have survived." I was told later in life that I was a happy contented baby that would sleep the day away if there was a radio playing in the room.

A Man About Town At Four

My earliest memories are when I was about age four. Our family was moving out of the little house in Carleton Lot Six and into what was called the Bloyce house in O'Leary. I guess we moved to O'Leary because my dad was working at the Co-Op Garage and my sister was working at Kennedy's store.

I became friends with a boy my age named Ralphie Silliker and we were for the most part inseparable. Our usual routine was for Ralphie to come over to my house in the morning, and then for the two of us to make our way over to the store (Kennedy's) to buy animal crackers (cookies that came in a cracker-jack-sized box in the shape of various animals). We loved animal crackers as well as the prize that came in every box (a little plastic railroad train car that would hook together with cars that came in other boxes). We would eat animal crackers until they came out our ears and stashed every car that came in the boxes in our pockets until we could get them to the safety of home.

Before we would ever consider heading for home, we had to complete our morning tour of the village. Mr. Pate, (Jack) the meat shop owner was always good for a friendly hello. Then the barber with his shop by the railway tracks would regularly acknowledge us with a wave of his scissors through his big front window with the barber's pole painted on it. We would bypass Jelley's furniture store and the Co-Op Store in favour of the Co-Op Garage with the big *White Rose* sign where my dad worked.

After a quick hello to my dad, we would head back toward the train station to spend the rest of the morning watching the train shunt and shove freight cars onto the side spurs to have

them loaded or unloaded as the need would have it. Almost everything of any size came and went by rail in those days.

Small freight to stores was sometimes delivered by transfer truck on weekly runs from Charlottetown all the way to Tignish. On the side of those green, three ton transfer trucks was a large yellow circle with the word **GRAY'S** in green letters painted like a Bayer's Aspirin logo. Yes, there was a family connection but we will leave that story for another day.

After a full morning of village touring and train-watching, my friend Ralphie and I would head back to my house where my mom would have lunch waiting, something good like tomato soup and a sandwich along with a tall glass of cold milk.

Lunch completed, Ralphie would head for home for his nap and I would find my own bed, crawl in, and close my eyes. I was out usually till almost three (about two hours).

On rainy days, our routine would be different. Ralphie and I would play train at my house with all of the little cars that we had collected from the animal cracker boxes. Our house had an adjoining kitchen, dining room and front hall in such a way that we could pull and push our trains of sometimes thirty, forty, or fifty little cars right around in a circle.

Playing train was one of my happiest memories of childhood. With Ralphie, every day of playing train was a happy day except on the rare occasion when someone happened to be coming through the house, back door to front door, didn't see our train, and walked on a section of it. Ouch! That would usually produce a half dozen or so casualties (little cars). But once the broken cars were removed and the two good ends reattached, we were back in the train business again. We would be able to start replacing the broken cars with new ones from our daily animal crackers boxes on our very next morning of village-touring and train-watching.

When I think back, it was a wonderful time that we lived in. A time when two four-year-olds could be let wander around the village for an entire morning without parents having to worry about us. I think that being a *man about town at four* produced a positive effect that I have carried with me throughout my entire life.

Sweet Smelling Memories of My Youth

When I was a young boy, quite a few years ago, my mother would dry the flannel sheets out in our back yard. Three lines ran between our house and the barn, and she would have all three filled with these sheets.

In winter, the damp sheets would freeze into semi-hardened shapes with interesting puckers where they were attached to the line with the clothes pins.

It was my chore to go out and retrieve these frozen sheets and bring them back into the house. Mom would construct a make-shift clothes-horse from high-backed wooden chairs, and drape the sheets over it. Our space heater would begin the drying process, and when they were fully dried, the sheets would then be deployed back to the various beds in the house. I have always loved the smell and feel of freshly washed flannel sheets.

I never could understand why Mom would hang the sheets outside in the winter. But since then, I have learned that the frosty air would cleanse the sheets of any little unwanted micro-organisms that may have survived through the washing process. Maybe that is why they always smelled so fresh and clean.

Looking back, I'm glad I never shirked my duty to retrieve the frozen sheets from the line.

Sheets on the Line

The Moving of Our House

The moving of the house occurred two years before I was born.

A crew of men used four foot logs, placing each in rotation before two skids installed under the house. A bulldozer with chains attached would pull the skids up and over the logs, allowing the house to move forward. It was a slow process, but eventually our house made its way from a back road in Coleman to a small plot of land on the Western Road bought by my father from Jake Mac-Naught.

My mother, sister, and grandmother remained inside the house as it rolled along on its way to the new location. They later would recount that the two most fearful moments were coming down MacNaught's Hill at the end of the Coleman road, and crossing the old bridge over the Trout River. They said that all they could see was the water, as the house hung over the small bridge on both sides.

An Old Farm House at Little Sands

Breakfast!

I am sitting at the kitchen table patiently awaiting your arrival there. Breakfast!

The most important meal of the day. Fresh coffee awakens my senses, filling them with the wonderful aroma that beckons forth the body to receive its morning jolt of Java. The sound of bacon and eggs in the pan, is like gentle rain on a metal roof. The familiar "pop" as the toaster releases its grip on two slices of whole wheat bread after toasting them to a golden brown. The sound of fresh orange juice pouring into a tall cold glass tumbler placed with its compliments of china plate, cup and saucer, silver knife, fork and spoon, cotton place mat and napkin on a sturdy wooden kitchen table.

I will visit with you, consume you, and savour you, as my body becomes enveloped with the warm satisfying awareness of having enjoyed you to your fullest.

Ready For Breakfast

Fall is Passing

Now, I am prepared to head out, ready to devour the day with its crisp bright sunshine, scarlet and gold leaves still on the trees, potato harvesting crews and machines working the red clay fields.

The last sail boats are being reluctantly plucked from the water on the Montague waterfront. The usual band of retired old guys, gathering at *Tim*'s to share an afternoon coffee and a yarn or two.

The shadows hint of the lateness of the day. I must head home to prepare my supper and watch a half hour of *Compass*, before I set out on my evening walk, read a chapter or two of my current paperback, and get ready to turn in for the night. The wind has picked up with the darkness that has fallen, and a cold dismal rain has begun to fall.

Strong is the wind—it tears the colours from the trees, until only the bare limbs, starkly proclaim in protest their nakedness, as they await the first covering of snow.

Fall is passing, winter is coming....

A Favourite Quote

A favourite quote of mine is: *"Time and unforeseen occurrence befall us all."* [1]

I love that quote because I am not a believer in predestination.

Contemplate seven billion, (with a *b*, give or take a few hundred thousand) human beings weaving their threads of life at any given moment on this earth. Being born, living, working, playing, suffering and dying. Like dust on the mantle or dew on a flower. Like a morning mist we are and then we are no more. It may seem impossible to find answers to our life's questions.

Wise King Solomon wrapped it up in *"The conclusion of the matter, everything having been heard, is: Fear the true God and keep his commandments. For this is the whole obligation of man."* [2]

As a God-fearing, with a healthy fear, human, who believes in creation and a resurrection into a new heavens and a new earth, I enjoy the peace of knowing that there is a time for everything.

"For everything there is an appointed time, even a time for every affair under the heavens: a time for birth and a time to die; a time to plant and a time to uproot what was planted; a time to kill and a time to heal; a time to break down and a time to build; a time to weep and a time to laugh; a time to wail and a time to skip about; a time to throw stones away and a time to bring stones together; a time to embrace and a time to keep away from embracing; a time to seek and a time to give up as lost; a time to keep and a time to throw away; a time to rip apart and a time to sew together; a time to keep quiet and a time to speak; a time to love and a time to hate; a time for war and a time for peace." [3]

I was brought up in a family that believed in God and observed His word the Bible with deep respect.

Today I still try to love God and love my neighbour just like many other fellow Islanders do.

The Apostle Paul says, *"All Scripture is inspired of God and*

---

1. King Solomon in Ecclesiastes 9:11
2. Ecclesiastes 12:13:
3. Ecclesiastes 3:1-8

beneficial for teaching, for reproving, for setting things straight, for disciplining in righteousness"[4]

The point of my writing is that although there are the questions that we all ask from time to time like "how do you make sense of this stuff?" Many of the satisfying answers that we seek may be found within the pages of our very own "family Bible."

For example, read Hebrews chapter 11 for "Faith" or 1 Corinthians 13: 4-8 for "Love."

You too may find a favourite quote within the pages of your "family Bible."

A Road to Follow

---

4. 2 Timothy 3:16

Field of Lupines

Laura-Jane Koers

Laura-Jane Koers is an internet consultant and freelance writer. She has been featured on national radio, including CBC's *Definitely Not the Opera* and CBC's *Outfront*.

Originally from British Columbia, Laura-Jane and her husband had no ties to the Maritimes and had never set foot on Prince Edward Island. But in 2007 the couple sold their B.C. home, packed up their belongings, and drove across the country in the middle of winter. Destination? Whim Road, P.E.I.

Laura-Jane chronicled their adventuresome Winter journey from B.C. to P.E.I. on her blog, *Whimfield*.

Laura-Jane is a passionate people-person who loves meeting Islanders and hearing their stories. She continues to write about daily life on P.E.I. and invites you to join the conversation at www.whimfield.com.

The Inevitable Question

If you're new to P.E.I. like I am, you quickly become accustomed to being asked what brought you to the Island. The answer doesn't always come easily. When I was put on the spot with this question, I used to be lost for words. I'd ramble or stumble over my explanation. Over the course of time I became more and more comfortable with the question, and now the answer flows so naturally from my lips I could recite it in my sleep.

The first time I was asked why my husband and I moved to the Maritimes, I was in a hardware store. The friendly man at the checkout said, "I heard that you drove all the way from British Columbia to Prince Edward Island to live here year-round. What made you choose P.E.I.?"

I didn't know how to answer. Numerous reasons battled in my head, and I rattled off twenty reasons: the high price of property in urban B.C., my desire to live

Main Street Montague

in a rural area, my dreams of starting a home-based business, my love of open fields, and my husband's quest to learn more about agriculture. I went on and on.

When I finally paused for breath, the look on the man's face made me realize that he was trying *not* to say, "I didn't ask for your life story! I've got customers waiting!" I glanced over my shoulder and noticed that the checkout line behind me had doubled during the time it had taken me to answer his question. With my head down, I hurried out to the parking lot.

The second time the question came up, I was in a government office renewing my driver's license. Looking at my old B.C. license, the attendant looked up at me and smiled, "B.C. is a long way away! Why did you decide to come to P.E.I.?"

This time I was better prepared. I knew that she didn't need to hear my life story, so I smiled and replied, "Property is really expensive out west. The prices are far more reasonable here." And I left it at that.

I'd expected that my short, pat answer would suffice. But the previously-friendly attendant frowned and said, "Hmm." Judging by her change of tone, I realized that my short, quick answer didn't work either.

It's natural for people born and raised on the Island—and from away—to want to know why a young couple would head to the Maritimes when many others are heading in the opposite direction. I knew the question would come up again, so it was time to get my answer straight.

So what did bring me to P.E.I.? There are a hundred reasons, but I've learned not to share all of them at once! These days, when I'm asked the inevitable question, I'm prepared with a quick story that covers all the necessary elements.

"My husband and I were living in a tiny condo in a city in B.C. where the cost of living was very high," I grin. "We didn't consider ourselves 'condo-people,' and we knew we wanted to make some big changes. We wanted a healthier, quieter lifestyle. Here on P.E.I. we live on 60 acres, and we've just launched a web consulting business that we run from home. The Island has exceeded our expectations in every way. It's a beautiful place to live, and we love it here!"

I grin when I tell my story because I do love it here. Perhaps I love Prince Edward Island most of all because people here are friendly enough—and interested enough—to *ask* me why we moved here.

The Adventures of Pete Plath, Lobster

Like many new Islanders, I was invited to tag along during a lobster run on one fine early morning in June. I came home with a live lobster of my own, after an exciting day on the boat. Driving home with the live lobster beside me on the vinyl passenger seat, I wondered about the lives of lobsters; one moment they're crawling along the ocean floor and a few hours later they're traveling along the roads of P.E.I. As I looked forward to my impending lobster dinner (which was delicious) during this drive home, I was also inspired to write the following tale, which tells a lobster's story in his own words.

Right now you are meeting me, Pete Plath, at the lowest point in a lobster's life; I am on the bottom of the ocean, caged inside a wooden trap. I am a lobster, so I know all about traps. During my daily routine, occasionally I spot a trap in the distance and I just step around it. It's not complicated; lobsters just have to keep an eye out for traps, that's all.

The prevailing sense in the lobster community is that if you're absent-minded enough to wander into a trap, perhaps you weren't as smart a lobster as we'd once thought. However, I myself always maintained compassion for lobsters who get trapped. Trapped lobsters are not necessarily foolish lobsters; bad things can happen to anyone, although I certainly never dreamt that this would happen to *me*.

Here I am, caught in a trap at the bottom of the ocean. Why me? I am not an obnoxious lobster who eats sea thistle and stumbles back to his burrow on seven of his eight pleopods; they are usually the first to get trapped. I am not an old-timer who is losing his vision and navigating on antennae alone. *I* am a male in my prime.

I'm a wise, generous lobster who should live long and do good in the world. No, I never dreamt that my end would come like this—awaiting my fate inside a trap at the bottom of the ocean.

Growing up, we lobsters heard spine-tingling stories about the few lobsters who've been trapped, yanked out of the water, and have made it back to their ocean homes again. There is a common pattern to survivor stories; the lobster is in the trap and she waits in shudder-some terror. The trap is suddenly yanked with shocking

Lobster Trap on Deck

speed up to the surface, and the trap lands right up onto a boat. One of you humans opens the trap easily, and the lobster is either flung into a hard container or thrown back into the ocean.

What happens if the lobster *doesn't* get thrown back into the ocean right away? Nobody knows the answer, because none of those lobsters have ever made it back to the ocean to tell their story. And what about the lobster who *does* get thrown back into the ocean right away? After a while such a lobster's story gets longer and more elaborate. Eventually, the other lobsters roll their eyes at the lobster who can't stop talking about that time she got trapped and how she made it back to tell the tale.... I've been in this trap for about three hours. Since I've been trapped, a crab has accidentally stumbled in here, too. I tried to warn her, but I don't speak crab. I can't understand what she's saying, but she's upset. If we could communicate, I'd remind her that many crabs get thrown back into koers ocean immediately after they get hauled up— unlike lobsters, who rarely get thrown back. At least the crab's got a fighting chance.

After the crab finished crying, she returned back to normal

crab behaviour, which, I must admit, is quite unpleasant. You'd think that the crab would want to bond together through our common misfortune, but instead she's staring at me with suspicion.

Sure, I *could* eat her, but food is the last thing on my mind right now. The crab has cinched herself up against the netting on the other side of the trap. What kind of an arthropod makes time for crustacean hierarchies at a time like this? Crabs... I'll never understand them.

I, on the other hand, am losing my composure. At first, when I found myself trapped, I was heroically calm. I was self-reflective and appreciative of the life I had led. I thought about the circle of life. *I was ready to meet my maker.*

But then the crab arrived and started crying. Now it's her animosity that is getting on my nerves. The crab has upset the balance of my peaceful end. If I am going to die, hurry up already.

Catch of Lobsters

Oh no, it's happening! The crab and I are being hurtled toward the surface! Wait a minute, Lobster Lord, I know I asked for this moment to hurry up and happen already, but I've changed my mind! I want to be back on the bottom of the ocean with the rude crab inside that tiny trap. Oh, please, no more! I'm not ready to die; I'm in my prime!

I'm exhausted. The humans yanked the trap up out of the water so fast that I think I've got the bends. My stomach feels topsy-turvy and my brain hurts. The crab got thrown back into the ocean—lucky broad—and now I'm on the boat in a plastic container, which is full of other lobsters; we're all squished together with very little personal space.

I thought I knew all the lobsters in this part of the ocean, but apparently I don't; they are all faces that I don't recognize.

Usually, I'm a patient lobster, but I am losing my cool. Plus, I happened to be placed right on top of a gorgeous lobster. I know I'm invading *her* personal space, but I've got nowhere else to move. And she's just my type, too.

Oh, how can I think about a woman at a time like this? What is going to happen *me?* Perhaps this is it; we're all going to die. I can't handle this... I just, oh, oh, oh...

I must have hyperventilated and passed out. I'm not sure where all the other lobsters went, but it's just me and one other lobster left in this container. The other lobster is the attractive lobster I was talking about earlier. I want to talk to her, but I don't have the strength. We're approaching land, and I can see a wharf of some kind. The boat has slowed to a steady chug, and I can feel myself dozing off again. I'm not fighting my urge to shut down.

I feel way better. There were a few sea urchins huddled in the corner of this container, and me and Wendl (that's the attractive lobster's name, so she tells me) ate a few of them. I feel re-energized and full of hope. I've been reassuring Wendl that we can get out of this situation.

Although we're trapped in this container, I can see water; the ocean is less than a foot below us.

Wendl and I have a plan: when a human sticks his hands inside this container, Wendl is going to distract him by running around in circles. Then, while Wendl's running and flapping her strikingly well-proportioned tail, I will grab one of the human's hands and pinch with all my strength. The best case scenario is that the human will be in pain, which will cause him to knock the container into the water. Our plan is highly possible. I mean, it *could* work. It might work. Oh man, who am I kidding, it's *not going to happen*. Wait, I can't be a pessimist. Wendl's counting on me; I've got to stay strong. I've got to have faith.

"Wendl, the human is coming! Get ready to move!" The human is above us; the human's hands are coming in. Wendl is running in bizarre circles, just like we planned. I am pinching the human's hand with all my strength. The container is teetering; our plan is working! The container is on its side, and we're sliding out of the container and into the water!

"Slide, Wendl, slide!" Wendl is making her escape; she is slipping out of the container, bouncing once along the edge of the boat, and plunging into the ocean! I'm sliding, too, and.... wait, no, no.... I'm *not* sliding, I am still pinching the human's hand. Now the human is grabbing me, let me go, let me go... I'm so close to freedom... No, no, *the human* has definitely got *me* now; he's sliding a rubber band around my claws. The human is putting me back inside the container. Wendl escaped, but I didn't. I'm still here, I'm still here.

I am in some kind of vehicle. It's bumpy and dark, and there are hundreds of lobsters in here. None of the lobsters are talking. We're all scared. I'm hungry again, and I can't stop thinking about Wendl. She was perfect. Even while she was out of the water she was beautiful in a natural, dry way. She believed in our plan, which made me believe in it, too. Wendl's probably making her way back to her home-town of Planktonia. A lobster like her won't stay single for long; she'll get married.

I'm sure she'll think of me fondly, though. She'll wonder why I didn't make it out into the ocean like she did. At least she made it; I saved her. Saving Wendl will be my legacy.

It's so bumpy in here. I wonder where we're going?

It took five days in a grocery store display case before we lobsters figured it out. At first, us naive crustaceans agreed that we must be entertainment. We had good reasons to believe this, too. My tank-mates and I were all fine specimens for our age (if I must admit, my left antenna is stunning), we were the only living animals kept in the whole store, and, when no one was looking, humans kept tapping on the glass. In many ways I warmed up to the idea of show biz; when I was a kid, I fantasized about joining the traveling invertebrate operettas. A life as a show-lobster might not be half-bad, I thought.

But then, yesterday, my fifth day in the tank, a human with a red-spotted apron plunged a pair of spiky tongs into the water and took one of my tank-mates, Alvin, away. Ten minutes later, we saw Alvin again. He was inside a clear plastic bag, being wheeled in a metal, four-wheeled cart. I don't know how Alvin found out, but as he was being wheeled by for the last time, he mouthed to us through the plastic bag: 'We're food! We are food!' Judging by the look in his eyes, Alvin was certain.

We were trying to look as glossy and appealing as possible when we thought we were entertainment. But now that we know we're going to be a main-course, we are trying to look as unappetizing as possible. We float around, giving blank stares and kinking our appendages in the wrong directions. Subtle misalignment of the ganglia seems to work well. Even so, every few days we lose a tank-mate or two to the human with the tongs.

I'm the only lobster left in this tank now. There's nobody for me to cheer up, and my spirits are failing fast.

Two weeks ago, when I was alone in that trap at the bottom of the sea, I came to terms with my own mortality. I'm trying to feel that peace and openness again, but, no matter how hard I try, I just feel scared, angry, and alone. I've stopped concentrating on how I look. I see now that it doesn't matter.

Everybody gets picked; it's just a matter of time. I've been using my time in this tank to reflect about my life and the events of the recent past.

I keep day-dreaming of how my life could have been if I'd escaped back into the water with Wendl. Would we have settled somewhere together and started a family? Right now, Wendl and I could be sitting at a friend's conch table, retelling our story of how, together, we'd escaped. Instead, here I am, alone in a tank, soon to become some human's dinner.

Well, it's happening, I can tell. An elderly lady is peering into my tank. She looks sad, but hungry. She's discussing something with the man in the apron. He's getting the tongs. I've seen it happen enough times now, so I know what to expect.

I'm sitting in a clear plastic bag, inside the elderly lady's car on the passenger seat. I'm beside a big fancy jar that is propped up very solidly, but I can't see what's inside it. The lady must really care about that jar, because she rests her hand on it—even while she's driving. She doesn't bother to look at me at all.

The car has stopped. The elderly lady has jammed me and my plastic bag into a backpack. She's wearing the backpack on her back, and it sounds like she's carrying that jar I was telling you about. She's been walking for a while. I don't know where we are, but we must be close to the ocean, because I can hear it. I'm trying to feel thankful for the chance to be near the ocean one last time, but it's hard.

I'm not ready to say goodbye. I can't help but feel resentful... My life wasn't supposed to end like this. I can hear the water loudly now. Dear Lobster Lord, thank you for letting me hear the ocean one last time... This isn't how I thought my life would end, but thank you for life. Thank you for letting me meet Wendl; she gave me hope. Thank you for my loving parents and for the happy life I did lead. I don't know what happens after death, but I tried to be good while I was alive. I hope that means something.

The lady has stopped walking. I still can't see anything because I'm inside the backpack, but I think we must be on a boat.

Strange irony, huh? Over the sound of the engine, I can hear the elderly woman talking to a younger man. They must be planning their meal.

The boat has been coasting along quietly for a while now. I'm still inside the clear plastic bag, but I can see the rest of the boat now that the man took me out of the backpack. The lady has been crying off and on, which seems strange. The younger man appears to be her son, and he's attending to her quite tenderly. He looks sad, too. But I'll tell you who's the saddest of all. Me. When are they going to eat me? Will it hurt? All this waiting is jangling my nerves.

The boat has dropped anchor in the middle of the water. The sun is starting to set and the view over the water is stunning. This appears to be our destination. I suppose now they'll cook me right on board. Yes, the young man is coming over to me now. He's undoing the clear plastic bag, picking me up gingerly, and putting me into a low-sided basket. I'm too tired to imagine escaping now. Plus, my claws were banded soon after I lost Wendl, so escape is not an option.

I'm in the basket and the man is unbanding my claws. They're about to prepare me for dinner, I suppose. But, oh, what divine freedom! Just to be able to stretch my claws one last time feels glo-

Murray River Lobster Boats

rious. While the man is unbanding me, the woman is still holding that jar I was talking about. Humans are very strange. Late night tank-talk revealed that the humans need a pot to cook me in. Where's the pot, anyway? I feel sick.

The man and woman are standing near the edge of the boat, looking over the water. The man is holding me now, and I am still completely unbanded. I could try to pinch his claws, but I feel weak. Besides, I could be crazy but I think he's considering letting me go into the ocean. I know how delusional that sounds, but I can't explain it; I think he's considering letting me go. Or else it could be some cruel joke. Perhaps they think I'll taste fresher if I've had a seawater rinse. Should I try to pinch him? This could be my only chance! Something tells me to act very still.

The woman has stopped crying and she's taking the lid off the jar for the first time. She leans forward and tips the jar upside-down over the water. Something grayish-white in colour and talc-like in texture spills out. As she empties the jar into the open water, a tear rolls down her cheek.

At the same time that the woman is shaking the last of the

jar's contents into the water, the man is gently lowering me down into the cool, velvety ocean. I'm half-submerged! His fingers are still around me, and my tail is starting to thrash. The man squeezes me a little and then quickly lets go and releases me.

I'm free—untethered, unbanded.... I'm under the water, traveling quickly down to the bottom, toward home.

Montague Harbour

Hugh MacDonald

"Most days of our lives, we are painting an image of ourselves. That's why the world is such a beautiful place." MacDonald, who lives with his wife Sandra in Brudenell, is a retired English teacher and a descendant of one of Canada's Fathers of Confederation. Many people know him, however, as raconteur and heritage enthusiast associated with the Roma at Three Rivers site, at Brudenell Point.

He authored *Chung Lee Loves Lobsters*, a child's book which won him a P.E.I. Literary Award in the children's literature category. He also won the Atlantic Poetry Award for his works. His poetry books include *Looking for Mother, The Digging of Deep Wells, Tossed Like Weeds from the Garden*, and *Cold Against the Heart*. His latest venture was to write a "junky page-turner novel" entitled *Murder at Mussel Cove*, which is becoming a hot seller locally and is also available at www.amazon.com web site.

He edited *Letting Go—An Anthology of Loss and Survival, A Bountiful Harvest—15 Years of Island Writing*, and *Landmarks—Writings from Atlantic Canada*. His own works appear in some twenty anthologies.

Together with P.E.I.'s Poet Laureate David Helwig of Eldon and the late Joe Sherman of Charlottetown, MacDonald formed *Saturday Morning Chapbooks*, an Island publishing firm that produced nine publications over a three-year period.

Hugh has always been ready for a challenge or an interesting diversion. He is a regular participant in the nationwide project entitled *Random Acts of Poetry*, treating members of the public to impromptu readings and free copies of one of his books.

And Gretsky and Me

*I'm off to play hockey
but I really think
my dad is the reason
we go to the rink.*

*He's doing the driving
with Mum at his side,
our great dog Gretsky
is along for the ride.*

*And dad is reminding me
how I should play.
He says the same thing
most every day.*

*My mom is done knitting
my new hockey sweater
and dad raves on about
how to play better.*

*He says if I listen
and learn to play well,
I'll score lots of goals
in the NHL.*

*He can brag to his buddies
and the guys at the bar
that his flesh and blood
is a great hockey star.*

*Before we leave home
I check on my gear.
I glance in the bag
Say, "I think it's all here."*

My socks are spotless
I have a new stick,
my brand new shin pads
are shiny and thick

And tonight at the game
as I go through my paces,
I'll skate even better
with my NHL laces.

So when we arrive,
I hurry right in.
I'll put on my gear
so the game can begin.

My dad lugs the bag,
does a happy dad dance.
He buys 50/50's
though he hasn't a chance.

The team is excited
and most are half dressed.
I open my hockey bag
to catch up with the rest.

I pull on my cup
get my garter belt on,
tape up my shin pads
till the tape is near gone.

Put on the worn stockings
that used to be Dad's,
hockey pants, neck guard,
elbow pads, shoulder pads.

Then the new hockey shirt
Dad says it looks great.
That's when I discover
I've forgotten a skate.

*My father is flustered
he's beginning to pout.
He looks through the bag,
tosses all my junk out.*

*He looks and he looks
half expecting to find it.
There's only one glove,
but he still looks behind it.*

*All of my teammates
file out of the room.
I sit with my dad
in the dressing room gloom.*

*He looks at his watch,
minutes left to game time.
Half an hour to home.
driving back the same time.*

*The game will be over
by the time he gets back.
His eyebrows look stormy
all bushy and black.*

*It is a safe bet
I will shortly get heck.
He glares and he snorts,
"Thought I told you to check."*

*Just at the moment
Mom comes through the door.
Dad snaps, "How many times
have I told you before."*

*"It really bugs me
when our son doesn't think.
So let's take him home,
get away from this rink."*

But Mom just stands there
with one of those faces,
and says, "Was it you
that put in his new laces?"

Then Dad turns around
with a deep furrowed brow.
He looks like a drift
in the path of a plow.

He lowers his head
and he lets out a groan.
"I set one skate down
as I answered the phone."

So I take my gear off
and we make our way out.
But as we go out the door
I hear someone shout.

"I'll lend you my skates.
I'm done for the day.
So if they're your size,
you can still get to play."

It is Suzy McGregor
which suits me just fine,
as long as her feet
are the same size as mine.

With Gretzky beside me
I fasten those blades
and burst out on the ice
and they feel tailormade.

I hear my dad cheering.
I tweak the twines twice.
and Gretzky goes crazy
like a cat among mice.

*So we are all happy
as we turn into our lane.
Gone is the tension,
the stress and the strain.*

*Father is cheerful
recalling my goals.
Gretzky is thinking
of dog treats in bowls.*

*Mother is happy
My new sweater fits right.
And I have decided
tonight is the night.*

*I state out loud
for my father to hear,
"There's worse things in life
than forgetting your gear.*

*"So I'll play hockey
so long as it's fun.
And I'll let you watch me
'cause I'm a good son.*

*"But if it's too painful,
I'm real sorry, Pop,
today is the day
I'm going to stop. "*

*My dad nods his head
and so does my mother.
We do a group hug
'cause we love one another.*

*We order a pizza
since we all agree,
my mom and my dad
and Gretzky and me.*

Tom Rath

Originally from Southwestern Ontario, Tom first moved to the Island in 1979, and lived in Charlottetown for two years before being posted abroad.

Following postings in England and Chicago, and several years in Ottawa, Tom took early retirement and moved once again to the Island.

During a ten-year period as Innkeeper of Lady Catherine's Bed and Breakfast, he welcomed thousands of overnight guests to his adopted P.E. I.

Tom is an active participant in an eclectic mix of trade and community organizations, and has been named the Eastern Prince Edward Island Chamber of Commerce's Member of the Year, and the Tourism Industry Association of Prince Edward Island's Operator of the Year. He has published *Lady Catherine's Kitchen, You're An Islander,* and *The KittenCat Adventures*.

He now resides in Upton, about twenty minutes from Montague, with his wife Fran and their cat, Black. He enjoys creative and non-fiction writing, and his works appear in several Island publications. Other interests include photography and cooking.

Come Lady

I am standing by the front window, looking out at a bright morning sky, watching waves on the shining blue waters of the Strait as they go rolling by.

The sun rises up past the shoreline, turning clouds every colour but white, and I think to myself, "Yes it's morning — and the world is still turning out right".

Come, Lady. Dance with me this morning, on grass cool and sparkling with dew. Come, Lady. Dance to a day yet a-borning, like this love growing in me for you...

There's a long red clay road going nowhere, and it stretches for many a mile. There's a halo of white sandy beaches circling round our dear Prince Edward isle.

I will walk with you down fields and pathways. I will stroll with you down every shore. We will wave back to Panmure Light's welcome, and we'll stay here, my love, evermore.

Come, Lady. Dance with me this morning, on grass cool and sparkling with dew. Come, Lady. Dance to a day yet a-borning, like this love growing in me for you...

When the stars in the Heavens grow weary, and they drop to the earth with a sigh, when the moon hanging over the water starts to cool and grow dim in the night—

Yet I'll stand by the window at daybreak, and I'll thank the good Lord for each day, And I'll turn to my darling and reach out. I'll take your soft hand and I'll say,

Come, Lady. Dance with me this morning on grass cool and sparkling with dew. Come, Lady. Dance to a day yet a-borning, like this love growing in me for you....

Fishing Boats

It's Autumn, and the fishing boats are resting in the yards, staring out across the fields, down and past the ruddy shore of Northumberland, the Strait where every Spring they will return for another year of fishing off the banks of P.E.I.

Their holds are filled with memories of lobster, crab and such, and all that they have gathered from the sea in years gone by. Then carried back to shore and given up to someone's shack to be sorted, weighed and packaged up for tables far away.

Oh, take me back to P.E.I., where fishing's in my blood,
To that isle of bright blue waters and its shores of reddish mud.
I'm like the salmon who has been too many years away.
I must hurry back to P.E.I. and it's here I must remain.

It's Winter, and the fishing boats are covered up in white. Fields are blown and salted with the snow that drives so hard. The only sounds you hear all day are winds that roam the sand and carry back the fragrance of the fair Northumberland.

But Spring will come again. When the ice has gone away, these fishing boats will leave their fields and travel to the Strait. They'll open up their holds for all Northumberland provides. Prince Edward Island fishing boats, they're very proud to be.

Oh, take me back to P.E.I., where fishing's in my blood,
To that isle of bright blue waters and its shores of reddish mud.
I'm like the salmon who has been too many years away.
I must hurry back to P.E.I. and it's here I must remain.

Catch at Weigh-in

Graham's Pond

Standing alongside the weigh-in,
watching the fishers unload
canners and markets a-plenty,
fresh from the salty and cold.
Laughter and banter around us,
for hardworking though they may be,
they still took the time to share greetings—
Our neighbours, the men of the sea.

We went walking along Graham's Pond,
to watch all the boats coming home.
We built a memory I now think upon,
of the days that we called all our own.

Tom Rath: Graham's Pond

You later found work in the factory,
for fishing was better than now.
You worked every day on the tables
while I stayed home working the plough.
Our babies came shortly and many,
and then grew as quickly as weeds.
and soon each was walking with lovers
to Panmure and Poverty Beach.

And they'd go walking along Graham's Pond
to watch all the boats coming home.
They built their own private memories
of the days they could call all their own.

Now, in the cool of the evening,
I sit on the verandah swing.
I think of the pond and of laughter,
and the day that I gave you my ring.
You'll always be here right beside me,
you'll always be sharing my bed.
I'll always remember your laughter;
I treasure the day we were wed.

I still go walking along Graham's Pond
to watch all the boats coming home,
thinking of memories we built way back when,
in the days that we called all our own.
I still think of memories we built way back then—
in those days that we called all our own.

Incident at Cape Bear

I certainly won't forget that night, let me tell you!

It happened not that long after I became Chief Operator, here at the Marconi station in the spring of 1912. Cape Bear was one of 22 stations scattered across the Eastern coastline. Our job was to handle communications between the shore and the ice-breakers, basically. Occasionally, you'd hear a distress message, but most nights were fairly routine.

My office was in the Southeast corner of the building, and I could look over there, to where the lighthouse used to be back then. That's what I was doing that Sunday night.

Beth had taken our children to bed hours ago, and I was working here in the office, and happened to glance out the window. It was a clear night, and you could see past the ice out in the Strait to the Nova Scotia coastline.

Over at the lighthouse, they were rewinding the big chain

Cape Bear Light (moved)

that makes the light revolve. They had to do this every four hours, so somebody was usually awake over there.

All of a sudden, this message started up. I wrote down the words, read them again, and said to myself, "No. This can't be!"

The message was that the new Titanic ship had hit an iceberg out on the Atlantic, and needed immediate assistance from anyone in the area.

Now I knew, just like everybody else did, that the Titanic was unsinkable. Why, that's what they wrote in the newspapers. There was just NO way that ship could go down. And so I wondered to myself if this weren't somebody's idea of a practical joke.

It wouldn't make any difference, of course. Joke or not, my responsibility was to pass that message on immediately to Charlottetown. And so that's what I did, just seconds later.

You know, in two hours, that unsinkable ship was deep underwater, 95 miles off the Grand Banks of Newfoundland. Imagine that. Over 2500 people on board for its maiden voyage from Southampton to New York, and hundreds of those people lost their lives. I tell you, my blood ran as cold as the water out there where she sank.

Not too long after, they told me that mine was the very first station in Canada to receive that distress signal. Well, I surely do hope my relaying it so quickly helped some. Because it was a terrible, terrible thing.

The Titanic

Mugs of Tea

*He is sipping his first mug of tea
looking out at a sky overcast.
Lobster boats are already at sea,
for his days as a fisher are past.*

*He remembers the wind and the smell and the rain
and the pull of the ropes that would make his back strain.
Those hands more than one lobster's claw have torn up
Now are warmed by the heat of his cup.*

*He is sipping his next mug of tea
in a booth, shared with old men who chat
of the weather, and tourists and boats,
but his mind still keeps drifting on back.*

*He remembers the wind and the smell and the rain
and the pull of the ropes that would make his back strain.
Those hands more than one lobster's claw have torn up
Now are warmed by the heat of his cup.*

*The day passes slowly, and yet
the years went by so quickly, you see.
Now he sits in his kitchen at night,
and he sips at that last mug of tea.*

*He remembers the wind and the smell and the rain
and the pull of the ropes that would make his back strain.
Those hands more than one lobster's claw have torn up
Now are warmed by the heat of his cup.*

Muddy Road

When springtime comes and tires get stuck
We curse the Island mud,
And yet we bless the same red soil
That grows the Island spud.

In a Potato Field

Outwitting the Feds

Fisheries Officers aren't always that high on the totem pole, in certain parts of Prince Edward Island, even if we all know they are basically good people. The thing is, when it comes to rules, many a fisher likes to decide for himself just how rigidly they should be followed. And as for that limit of 300 lobster traps, well, not everyone can even count that high.

These two fishers, for example—perhaps their names were Roger and Edgar. They used to row out to this particular spot where a couple of unauthorized traps were located. Roger and Edgar considered they weren't really breaking the law; after all, they just enjoyed their feed of P.E.I. lobster.

Of course, Fisheries Officers don't see things the same way at all, you realize, so when they heard about those traps, they hid one evening around the point, in their great big boat with the twin motors.

However, Roger and Edgar had learned in advance that the Fisheries Officers were laying in wait, so what they done was this. They tied one end of a rope to the back of the rowboat, and the other end onto Edgar's Jeep. The plan was right simple. If Roger gave the signal, Edgar was to jump into the Jeep and take off down the road into the bush, dragging the rowboat back to shore before Roger could be caught.

As it turned out, the plan worked.

Roger was right by the traps when the Fisheries boat came a-roaring around the Point so fast that the prow was clear out of the water, thanks to those big motors. Roger immediately waved his oars in the air, and started pretending to paddle back to shore.

Seeing this, Edgar took off in the Jeep, making that rowboat literally skip across the waves. Apparently Roger was afraid to let the oars actually touch the water in case they snapped right off from the speed.

What neither one had thought about, of course, was exactly how far from shore Roger was at the time, and therefore, exactly when Edgar should stop driving away.

You can picture what happened. As soon as the rowboat hit

the rocks, it burst into a shower of splinters.

Surprisingly, Roger didn't get more than a bruise, and a scrape or two. And he said later that it was worth everything just to see the astonished faces of those Fisheries Officers as he sped away from that powerful boat of theirs.

Hills and Harbours

The hills and harbours beckon me,
  and no matter where I roam
I still feel insistent yearnings,
  telling me to come back home.

Prince Edward Island's not my birthplace
  but it's home inside my heart.
When those hills and harbours get you,
  you can never really part.

You can travel the world over
  but you'll never get away.
When those hills and harbours beckon
  here's the place you'll want to stay.

Hot September Evening Sky

The haze has lifted. Nova Scotia's
* a dozen miles across the Strait.*
And in the sky, toward that coast,
* geese practice wings and calls, in wait.*

This summer has been hard on crops—
* too dry. "Not so!", would say my guests,*
who know not what the fall will bring.
* Perhaps, perhaps that's for the best.*

And me? I watch the water change
* to complement the sky.*
And listen by the phone each night,
* for who may call, from where, and why.*

Tom Rath: PEI Stew

PEI Stew

I'm not fancy, I'm not proud,
don't worry my head wanting more than what's allowed.
There is one little thing, though, that I wish you would do.
Please fix me up a bowl of that PEI stew.
Lots of mussels, heaps of clam -
It's a happy man I am.
Throw some lobster in there, too.
Now you're cooking PEI stew!

It's a rich taste, quite easily acquired.
It's a flavour of which I never will get tired.
Spread some butter upon a home-baked biscuit or two
to sop up all the juices of that PEI stew.

I say no thanks to every steak that I find.
You can keep your French cuisine. No - I don't much mind.
Save it for others, for it just will not do.
All I really want's a bowl of PEI stew.
Sure I'll eat salad, and I don't mind those greens.
I'll finish up my turnip, and all of my beans.
I'll clean up my plate, eat what you want me to.
Just as long as you can serve it with some PEI stew!

It's a fine taste, and one that pleases me
It's a wine taste, a wine right from the sea.
There's no flavour like it. No other dish will do
like a heaping big bowl of PEI stew!

Storm

The anger of the rolling waves made caps of knuckle-white.
The seagulls all had flown away, escaping from the sight.
Escaping from the furious, and leaving bare a shore
Of sand and seaweed, shells and stones, and footsteps from my door.

Ignoring slap of wind-tossed rain, and wind that leaned so hard,
Ignoring cold that pierced my neck, as sharp as any shard.
I strode a mile, another, three, along that wretched beach.
I sought safe harbour from myself—a harbour out of reach.

And then at last the storm gave up, and slowly went away.
I turned to walk back home again, and face another day.
My anger too had lost its strength, but like that pelting rain,
It left its mark on eyes and heart still echoing with pain.

Stormy PEI Shore

Red Plaid Vest

I was just a young'un, I don't recall my age.
I'd sit and watch my Daddy playing up there on the stage.
Every jig and reel and air showed he was the very best.
But what I most recall was seeing Daddy's fancy red plaid vest.

I dreamed that someday I could fiddle tunes the way he did
Playing music for our grown-up friends and all us kids.
I practiced to be good enough and one day passed the test.
I played alongside Daddy and his trademark red plaid vest.

Years went by and Daddy's fingers grew so stiff that he
Could only sit down there in front, to watch and smile at me.
I played to many audiences from north, south, east and west,
Who came to watch me fiddle in my Daddy's red plaid vest.

Daddy's gone now and he's found a better place to play
And though I miss his smile and tenderness each day,
Every night I listen to him as I get my rest
Through the pillow that I made from Daddy's red plaid vest.

Donkey Oatie's Impossible Dream

Oatie was just a little donkey. Not much taller than the grass in some of the fields he explored each day. When the sun got hot enough and his head drooped with the need for a nap, you sometimes didn't see him at all.

But Donkey Oatie had a dream. An impossible dream, some might say.

Donkey Oatie wanted to be a cow.

You see, Oatie wasn't the only animal out there in the green fields just past Maggie's Restaurant in North River, PEI.

Now and then, Oatie had seen some larger animals roaming, and grazing, and enjoying the sunlight. They had big bodies, big heads, and big, gentle eyes.

At first, he was a little unsure of whether or not they were friendly. After all, they were much bigger than he, and there were so many of them and just one of him.

One day, however, he finally got up the nerve, and walked over to say hello. When he did, he discovered something else. These larger animals didn't sound like him, either. They made low rumbling moo sounds—friendly sounds, admittedly, but different.

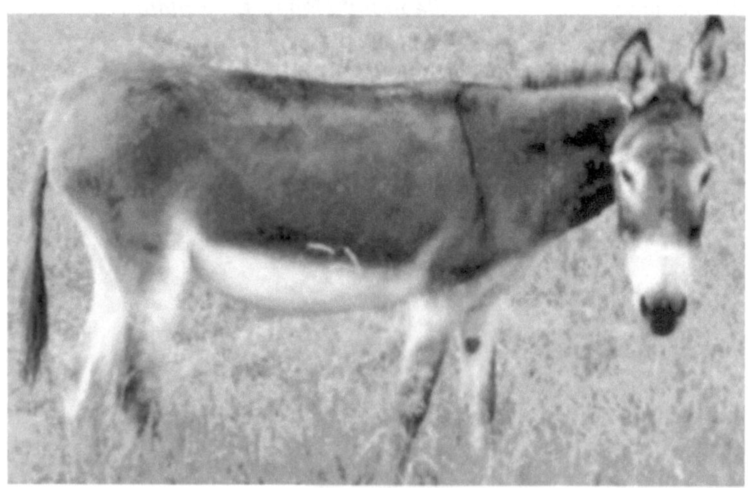

Donkey Oatie

They didn't seem to mind him coming so close, perhaps because there were so many of them. They just continued to chew at the grass, and to gaze at him with their big, gentle eyes.

Oatie felt quite at home with his new friends. It felt good. He wished he were a cow.

One day, he stood beside a young calf that, for a change, wasn't being as frisky as usual. The youngster was just nibbling at the grasses, its head down to the ground. As Oatie glanced over at the youngster, he noticed a sudden movement just behind them both. It was a hungry animal with pointed ears and a mouth full of sharp teeth.

As the coyote took a leap into the air towards them, Oatie kicked back with his powerful back hooves, and the predator was thrown tumbling head over heels, landing back in the grass with a painful thump. The coyote scrambled to his feet and dragged himself as quickly as possible back across the field toward the trees.

Seconds later, one of the big cows came running over and checked out her young calf, relieved to see there was no injury. The cow stared at the donkey with big, gentle eyes, and both of them knew that even if Oatie wasn't really a cow, he would always be welcome to walk in the fields with his new friends.

The next time you're in North River, take a look across the fence, and you might see Oatie, watching you.

Donkey Oatie had an impossible dream, but in a way, it came true that day.

An Island Ceilidh

On many a summer evening, one hears from various rural community halls the strains of a fiddle and accompanying piano, the energetic clatter of stepdance shoes on a wooden stage, and the friendly applause of audiences hearing the old stories recited once again. It's a traditional gathering on Prince Edward Island, and one of the best ways to end the day.

To visitors from away, *Ceilidh* is just a word whose odd spelling offers no clue as to how it might be pronounced or what it might represent. To Islanders and others in the know, Ceilidh rhymes with daily, and is a Gaelic word which originally referred to the kitchen parties so common in years gone by.

The big kitchen in many farmhouses is where families would spend much of their time. After supper, Uncle Joe might come over with the fiddle, Mom might tell the kids to "Get up there and dance!", and an enjoyable evening of story-telling would be had by all, punctuated by a "lunch" of sandwiches, squares, and hot tea served midway through the proceedings.

Nowadays, the party has moved to larger facilities, to accommodate a typical audience of 100 Islanders and visitors, all eager to hear area singers, fiddlers, and storytellers, and to watch young dancers demonstrate their talented footwork.

Among the oldest of these gatherings is Ceilidh at the Hall, a Wednesday evening highlight for the past quarter century at Orwell Historic Village, twenty minutes east of Charlottetown. Another popular venue is the BIS, or Benevolent Irish Society, on North River Road in Charlottetown. On most nights of the week, anyone across the Island can find a Ceilidh within easy driving distance.

Surprising to first-timers is that so-called "lunch", still served at many Ceilidhs midway through the evening, and often included in the $5 to $10 price of admission. At some venues, it might consist of actual sandwiches, tea and squares, or be a more modest offering of home-baked biscuits and jam.

At Orwell, lemonade and tea are complimentary, while an additional charge brings an ample serving of strawberries and ice cream.

Another surprise is the typical invitation at some locations to participate in the program, which gives regular attendees a chance to hear new voices and instruments.

The final surprise is old hat to regulars, but never fails to draw gasps from newcomers to the Island.

Stepping out of a country hall on the island at 10 p.m., one can look up to a magnificent display of constellations and the occasional satellite, lighting the way back to the car, and igniting dreams and memories of a summer visit to Prince Edward Island.

Music Group With Percussion Section

Grandpa's School

Grandpa took me to his school. It's old, but lots of fun.
Six windows and two wooden doors. A big bell hangs by one.
A real fat stove is sitting in the middle of the floor.
The job of starting fires went to the first one through the door.

The whiteboard isn't white at all, but sort of grayish black.
The alphabet's along the top, there's brushes on the track.
His teacher's desk is made of wood just like the ones for kids.
But there's a funny little hole right there on all the lids.

Grandpa said the hole is for a bottle filled with ink.
He said that when they wrote, they used a quail, I think.
There is a bathroom for the girls, and one more for the boys.
I asked about computers, and where were all the toys.

He sort of smiled and said they didn't have things like that then.
And no TVs or even films to play there, way back when.
I asked if Grandpa liked his school, the way things used to be.
He shrugged and whispered those old days are very dear to me.

And then he said when I grow up in maybe fifty years,
I'll show my grandson my old school, and try to hide my tears.

You're An Islander

A short eleven months ago I moved here,
and left Toronto's city life behind.
I left the joys of Yonge Street in mid-Summer
and came to tiny Charlottetown to find—

A place where people smile and say, "Good Morning!,"
where neighbours know your name, and want to please,
where friendship is a thing you take for granted,
as common as Prince Edward Island breeze.

There's a gentle kind of people on the Island,
and a type of calm that washes like the tide.
The Mainland's far away, and if only for a day—
You're an Islander, and feeling good inside....

The Rest of the Story

Prince Edward Island is well-known for its summers, as a million or more tourists happily attest. What could surpass the appeal of sunny days, rolling landscapes, and a cornucopia of concerts, Ceilidhs, and community festivals? Who hasn't sat on a lawn chair in mid-August, to marvel at crystal-clear night skies glistening with stars and satellites?

Those of us fortunate enough to live here know there's so much more to Prince Edward Island. We don't tell everybody, but in case you weren't aware, dear reader – we've got three more seasons to enjoy on our Island.

Sit back and I'll tell you about the other nine months or, as the late Paul Harvey says, "Here's the rest of the story."

Autumn Leaves. Anticipation has elements of Nostalgia built right in, when you stop and think about it. Take autumn on Prince Edward Island, as an example.

We see those first few hints of gold and red in the roadside trees, and we look for more. Driving the hills and back roads of the Island, or strolling through the parks and woodlands, we eagerly seek out the brilliant shades that will soon be everywhere in great abundance.

We imagine ourselves as fine artists, capturing magical images to sustain us through the long winter months ahead. We spend scarce dollars on watercolour paints and brushes. We smell the morning air and vow to take long walks through favourite fields.

That's when it hits us.

Are we really looking forward to autumn? Or in truth, are we looking back upon years gone by?

Back when we, as children, scrunched our way through piles of dried leaves, kicking up flashes of faded glory. Back when we sat on the veranda and listened to Mom telling us about forest animals preparing for winter. Back to that day we stood and watched in awe as long V's of Canada Geese rowed their way across the sky, honking encouragement to each other. Back to the smells of ripening apples, baking pumpkin and roasting turkey.

Autumn on Prince Edward Island brings joyous memories of experiences shared with neighbours, friends and family. It uses sounds and colours and aromas and tastes and touches, evoking laughter in children and smiles in grown-ups. It reminds us all that seasons, like life itself, are cycles that will last an eternity.

Autumn arrives, and Autumn leaves.

An Island Winter. How best to describe an Island winter? In days gone by, or 'them times' as some would say, winter was much more a real season.

Back then, winter meant watching the horse-racing on the Hillsborough, after days of preparing both river surface and horse. Hot chocolate, warm clothing, and the ruddy complexion of faces entranced with excitement at the noise, the vibration and the sight.

Winter meant being storm-stayed for a day or two, hunched over the kitchen table in an avid challenge of crokinole. Hearty meals of root vegetables and meat, and evenings being entertained by velvety-voiced Eric MacEwen on CFCY, Don Messer on the black and white TV, and pictures of far-off places in *National Geographic* magazines.

Winter meant ice-fishing, skating on the pond, and horse-drawn sleigh-rides through the woods and fields, bundled under blankets and feeling the sharpness of a breeze that in other seasons was merely refreshing.

Winter meant learning about animal tracks, and rolling gigantic balls into a smiling snowman tall enough to guard the house from any predator.

Winter meant crafts, although they were less an avocation in those days, and more just a typical feature of rural life. Quilts were always being assembled, mittens always being knitted by the kitchen stove, for family Christmas gift-giving, not for selling to tourists somewhere on the Mainland.

Nowadays, winter is a sometime thing, hard to define, and hard to pin down. It's later than it used to be, with the odd snowfall or storm arriving in October or December, only to melt within a day or two. Some years, snow doesn't stay long on the ground until perhaps the end of January. A green Christmas isn't uncommon. On the other hand, an Easter morning could be bitterly cold and a bright white landscape that keeps you indoors searching for coloured eggs and chocolate.

Nowadays, many Islanders spend at least part of their winter in Florida, or North Carolina, or anywhere else than Home. Fewer games of crokinole are played, and more *Super Mario*. Fewer root vegetables are served, and more pizzas.

But in some hearts and memories, winter on Prince Edward Island is still a time for reflection, a time to re-establish bonds with family, friends, and neighbours. While you may no longer need snowshoes to stroll through the woods in winter, you still need a curious mind, an adventurous spirit, and an Island heart.

The Miracle of Spring. Spring is truly the most miraculous of seasons. At first, the seed of life's annual renewal remains hidden from our eyes. We see only bare branches on tired and worn-looking trees. Snow melts from our fields and lawns, revealing the stained and withered remains of last year's growth. Ice slowly recedes from waters whose dark turbulence induces an involuntary shiver.

And then the miracle occurs.

Once more, we watch fragile crocuses poke up through the remaining drifts of snow around our houses to proclaim through bright yellow and purple petals, "We are back!". Tufts of green unfurl on our trees, urged on by chattering birds eager to begin their nesting ritual. Neighbour fishers venture out into their yards, scraping down and repainting boats, repairing nets and traps, preparing for that first run into the Northumberland Strait and Gulf waters for lobster.

Winter tires are returned to the garage, together with shovels and snow-blowers, occupying space vacated by gardening tools and deck furniture hauled out for another year. In the house, spring cleaning becomes an irresistible priority, even for muscles out of tone from the winter months just past.

In kitchens across the Island, cookbooks and magazines are shuffled in anticipation of our cuisine evolving from hearty casseroles to more delicate soups, salads and entrees featuring newly-grown produce from Island gardens. Children put away their sleighs and mittens, and get out their bicycles, their marbles, their baseballs and their chalk, eager to explore that new world of a thousand greens and red, red soil.

Spring has returned to Prince Edward Island, and the world is indeed a beautiful place.

"…and now you know the rest of the story" (Paul Harvey, 1918-2009).

Spring View

Tom Schultz

While a professor of Electrical Engineering Technology at Purdue University in Indiana Tom Schultz was drawn, with his wife, to P.E.I. on a vacation about nine years ago. A few years later he retired so they could spend full time at their house in Wood Islands.

He started as a publisher by re-issuing a technical book he wrote while teaching. He subsequently released *Prince Edward Island; Seen 'From Away'*—a book he wrote about his experiences and impressions of P.E.I. He published *House of Angels* written by Loman Bell, an Islander from the Murray River area, and is writing a book about sailing. In addition to writing and publishing, he is active in photography, teaching a course on the subject at the Murray Harbour Community School and producing photo-products supplied to gift shops. Additional activities include sailing (the subject of one of these articles), Bible teaching, and forestry. He may be contacted at schultz@PEI.sympatico.ca

Boating For Fun

Kinds of Craft And Places To Go. Boating strictly for pleasure is relatively rare in the waters around P.E.I. Most boats around the Island are 42'- to 45'-long commercial fishing boats with a distinctive forward cabin and the wide, open deck area to the rear. The design is useful for processing any catch or holding the nets and traps—a work-boat layout.

I know of several Islanders who have converted older, retired fishing boats to pleasure use. Such boats, along with the working boats that have finished for the season, are drafted for use on Canada Day. Family and friends—even distant relatives and stray friends—all crowd onto the boat for festivities out on the water. The barbecue is brought aboard and fired up near the stern. All the working gear and tanks have been cleared away so there is plenty of room—lawn chairs are set up on the rear deck, and in the cabin there is a table with bench seats on both sides. There is the entire forward cabin with its bunks for the kids to explore and play in. The sounds of such parties echo across the harbours on those holidays.

The high cost of fuel to move these large fishing boats around limits travel. Lorin Panting guessed it cost him about $200 in fuel to take his fishing boat across from Wood Islands to Pictou Island and back. It is one thing to write such costs off against income from a lobster catch, but it is too expensive to motor around in those big boats just for the fun of it. Most of the converted fishing boats become sort of floating cabins by the shore, with folks visiting them as you might go to a cabin in the woods—bring along a supply of food and some good books, hang out for the weekend, and go home Sunday night. Oh, you might take the boat out for a few hours occasionally, but that is the limit of typical cruising.

Why are so few of the more flashy pleasure boats found outside of Summerside and Charlottetown? Perhaps only city folks choose to use spare income for such things. Coming across the Hillsborough bridge into Charlottetown in the summer—especially on weekends—I often see 10 or 20 small to medium-sized sailboats out in the harbour—perhaps participating in races or just enjoying a nice day on the water. George Power, a friend who keeps a mid-sized sailboat in one of the marinas in Charlottetown, introduced me to sailing. He'll go out at the drop of a hat with anyone who expresses an interest! Only on exceptionally warm days is it comfortable in the very small sailboats—the kind of sailboat where you can expect to be blown over by a gust of wind, swim around to the side, right the boat, and resume sailing. I have never seen small sailboats outside of the sheltered harbours of the two cities. That is the pleasure boat scene on P.E.I.

Sailboat at Wood Islands.

Let me describe how I fit into this picture. I own a 26' trimaran that is now the only sailboat—or pleasure boat of any sort—calling Wood Islands home. I bought it from John MacDonald who had it in Cardigan, but Terry Drake in Morel built it over two decades ago—I'm told for a professional person in Summerside. A trimaran is a three-hulled boat—a main hull and two narrow outrigger hulls all held together with beams.

Trimaran at Mooring

Mine has a wide deck across all three hulls. Construction is of plywood, glued and coated with epoxy which also attaches an outer covering of fibreglass. By epoxy-coating all the wood, it is preserved from rot and becomes surprisingly long-lasting even in salt water. The long-term durability of this construction technique was unproven some 22 years ago, but I am happy to report that it has held up at least as well as newer techniques. Enough about the boat.

Wood Islands Harbour on the southeast end of the Island is right on Northumberland Strait. Nowhere else on the Island is there the frequent traffic of two large ferries all summer. In addition, at least 20 fishing boats are based here—I'm not sure of the exact number in the water, but it starts high in lobster season (May and June) and then varies as the year progresses. Some fishing boats go back to the fisherman's yard as soon as lobster season has ended, but other boats remain in the harbour for various other fishing including herring and scallops. An occasional large sailboat stops by, spending the night at the wharf before continuing a long cruise—perhaps from Cape Breton or Montreal. I do see an occasional small powerboat launched from the ramp for the day—it usually races out to the Strait, runs around like an angry hornet, and comes back within a few hours.

I long ago determined that the best parking place for my sailboat is attached to a mooring block at the most sheltered region of the outer harbour. Just inside the 'steels' is a narrow, deep-enough strip between the deep channel used by the ferry and the shallows near the shore. At the wharf, my sailboat was in the way of the fishing boats. There is not enough space to fit each boat around the wharf so the boats are tied up one outside the next—3 or 4 boats deep. If my sailboat were tied on the outside, it would have to be moved repeatedly at 4am by the fishermen. On the other hand, it is too light to be sandwiched between the heavy fishing boats.

The Sailing Experience. Going out in my sailboat has many associated sounds and feelings that I'd like to describe. Come with me in my pickup as I drive around past the lighthouse to where the road ends at the steels. From there we can look out at the Strait and get an idea of the conditions we may face. Some days the water looks calm—will there be enough wind to sail? Other days it looks windy with waves breaking on the shore and lots of red-brown froth from where the waves have churned the bottom up just out from the beach. Is it safe to go out? The answer depends as much on the anticipated passengers as on the wind gauge reading on the boat. Experience has taught that winds over 25 knots, while not dangerous to the sailboat, make for a very uncomfortable ride suitable only for intrepid thrill-seekers. If a strong wind has been blowing along the Strait for some time, notoriously choppy waves develop to make any trip unpleasant. With a wind speed above 35 knots, even with the sails reduced, conditions develop that, though they can be handled by this boat, should be avoided by any prudent captain. Fortunately, such winds are rare— almost unknown during the summertime.

Having glanced at the conditions in the strait, look with me out at the boat at its mooring. I always have a little anxiety because several times the boat has dragged the mooring block a little ways—a few times it has broken loose and drifted across the harbour! Are there waves in the harbour with a wind that will make rowing the dinghy a big job?

Our next glance is to make sure the dinghy is still upside down in the grass. This has never happened, but someone *might* take it for a joyride. Is the tide low, so we have to drag the dinghy over the rocks or is it high, so we can launch from the sand and easily float over those rocks? Depending on the tide level, one of us may have to wade out to launch the dinghy beyond the rocks— you need boots, or a willingness to get wet feet. High tide is nice because the dinghy can be launched from a sheltered sandy cove, while low tide allows launching off the deeper rocks. At intermediate depth we have to wade through the water before there is enough depth to float.

Rowing 50 yards out to the sailboat is usually not difficult, but winds and waves can make the trip precarious if the dinghy is heavily loaded. There is not a lot of freeboard on the very small dinghy so we must be well balanced to keep the water out. The load limit is two heavy adults, so getting a number of people aboard requires multiple trips. Approaching the sailboat the oarsman must decide to head for the bow or the stern. Approaching from upwind, the dinghy can drift to the boat, while approaching from downwind means we will be sheltered as we unload. Too strong wind and the dinghy may blow past the sailboat—requiring a fierce rowing effort.

While this sailboat can be managed single-handed, it is much easier to have two—one to hold the tiller and another to work the sails. Getting on the boat is like visiting an old friend. I'm proud of improvements. Be patient with me while I take a minute to admire recent improvements. A quick glance in the bilge ensures there has been no leak or failure of the pump. I also check the battery voltage—it has run down when the pump switch stuck on or when lights were left on.

After the quick inspection below, let's make sure the outboard motor starts. With the wind out of the west, it is difficult to simply sail out. An energetic crew might enjoy the challenge to go out and return strictly by sail power, but when it comes time comes to stop playing around and get where you need to go, I want to be sure the motor works.

Let's raise the sails before we start out. To try that out on the Strait can be difficult because the sailboat may be pitching or we may not be facing directly into the wind—the orientation where the sails slide up easily. Besides, while still tied up to the mooring I can take time to explain what needs to be done. If we set the sails after we get out on to the open water, it is hard to hear in the wind and you may have trouble staying upright on the shifting deck. To set the sails, remove their covers, attach the *halyards* (nautical term for the ropes that attach to the top corners to lift the sails up) and *sheets* to the *jib* (the ropes that hold the back corner of the front sail), and I'll pull the sails up.

Next, one of us needs to unfasten the mooring lines. On short outings, I leave the dinghy tied to the mooring in place of the sailboat, so we need to switch the connections. Once we head out into the channel, I, the captain, carefully make sure not to catch the mooring line in the propeller—*usually* it will slice through a line, but even in that best of situations the float would drift free, leaving the mooring unmarked (Ask me how I know!).

Where is the ferry? Will we encounter it in the narrow passage between the steels? While there is technically enough room to pass the ferry there, I expect the ferry captain dislikes that since it forces his large boat closer to one wall of the passage as well as worrying about my doing something stupid. He has the right of way, being a large, less maneuverable vessel, but the marine rules require all vessels to do everything they can to avoid a

Crew at the Tiller

collision. Unfortunately, at the mooring we can't see if a ferry is about to enter until we move out into the channel, so that adds a bit of uncertainty. Under motor we can circle around if we must and stay out of the way, but with sail we would be less maneuverable.

Using the outboard motor, we can move along at about 6 knots—a comfortable speed. As we pass between the steels there is echoing off the sidewalls—especially if someone shouts—but most of our attention is on the waves and water up ahead.

Passing out of the channel into the Strait brings the real excitement—we find out for the first time how high the waves *really* are and how hard the wind is *really* blowing. With the shape of the shore and the tide pattern, the water just outside the steels at Wood Islands can be the roughest on the entire Strait. This first contact can be a shock. Have we made a big mistake in coming out and should we turn around? I usually run the motor long enough to clear the last channel marker buoy before shutting it off.

As the sound of the motor dies out, we experience the high moment of sailing. In the *sudden quiet*, you can hear the flap of the sails. You feel the swelling up-and-down motion that says the sail-boat is handling whatever waves are out there. To me it brings a sense of being able to master whatever conditions will arise.

We probably won't go anywhere on this outing. Most of the trips are just for fun to be out on the water for a couple hours with the sun and wind. Some days the wind turns out less than forecasted. A least one time, it was so calm we just anchored and went swimming out by the lighthouse. The real down side to water around P.E.I. is its temperature. It may be "the warmest water in eastern Canada," but that is not saying much. Swim-ming in open water, you will discover warm spots where the sun has been working, and a few feet over, cold spots where the tide churned up water from below. I insist life jackets be worn. One time the wind suddenly picked up and the furthest-out swimmers got to imagine what it would be like to be abandoned!

More Tiller Help

If there is a slight wind, we may still try to sail. The colourful, balloon-like *spinnaker* sail can help a little—at the least it gives the crew something to do as the sailboat sits almost still in the water. Then there are the time the wind just stops. Often the waves linger after the wind has died down. Then you sit there listening to the sails flapping back and forth as the bobbing of boat shifts the mast from side to side. It does give us an opportunity to talk and just sit

Young Passengers out Sailing

and relax, but it can be frustrating—especially if we went out in faith, trusting the word of the weather bureau.

On the other hand, there are days of ideal winds—10 to 20 knots are best. We then sail out on a *broad reach* (crosswise to the wind) or *point* as high as we can into the wind (about 45° off from straight into the wind—the best anyone can do on a sailboat without the engine). These medium winds are the most fun. The picture here shows a group of passengers. The younger ones seem to enjoy it most—I think they view it as a sort of amusement park ride. Being the captain carries a level of responsibility that tempers the fun with a concern for everyone's safety.

Most times we turn around after an hour or two because of someone's schedule or approaching twilight. As long as we were careful not to sail down-wind, the return trip can use the same wind that pushed us out, now on our other side, to push us back. As we get closer to the steels we look back to gauge the position of the ferry—can we get through before it arrives, or should we circle around for a while so it goes in ahead of us? As we are returning through the steels, we are lowering the sails and may even be putting the sail covers on. One of my regular crew members finds great joy in shouting out his favourite line, "Lower the jib!"

Once back through the steels, if we are still relying on the sail, we have to circle around the mooring float so that the boat faces into the wind to provide the 'brakes.' You can be up front with the boat hook to catch the rope that connects to the float while I try to bring the boat to a stop right at the mooring. Once you catch the line, quickly wrap it around a *cleat* (a two-horned fastening point) before the sailboat drifts away or overshoots the mooring. Incidentally, my first boat hook is somewhere down there in the mud because, despite stuffing its aluminum tube with Styrofoam, it sank when the inertia of the boat ripped it out of my grip! The new one is made from a cherry sapling from our woods—and, in advance, I tested to be sure it floated. After the initial tie to the mooring, we can relax. Let's finish putting the covers over the sails, make a firmer mooring connection, and gather up any stuff to go ashore.

After the boat is closed up, untie the dinghy and one of us can row any passengers, one by one, back to shore. Following a last look around, the oarsman and I go ashore, hoping that everything will remain in place until next week's outing.

One Lobster Fishing Trip

Basil Miller--Captain

As you drive around the Island, you will see numerous small harbours, usually with at least a few of the distinctive-shaped P.E.I. fishing boats nestled against the wharves. These boats have a distinctive high bow with bunks below, an enclosed cabin, and a low-sided, open rear deck where the processing takes place. Most fishermen don't mind you walking along the wharves and inspecting the boats. If they have finished work for the day and happen to be standing around, they may be willing to answer questions or chat about the world in general. Etiquette requires that you board a boat only by invitation, but there is no harm in asking.

A friend, Paul Badgley, got me an invitation to go along on a fishing run, so I can now write about lobster fishing from "first-hand" experience (if one trip can qualify). He crews out of North Lake (on the northeast end of the Island) on the *Miss PEI*, owned and captained by Basil Miller of Murray River. The plan is to meet at Poole's Corner at 3:30am, followed by an hour's drive up to the harbour. Jarred awake by my alarm, hauling on clothes and climbing into the cold car in the pitch dark, I get to the meeting place just in time. I readily agree to let him drive, since he knows the route. His car is warm and secure, and it is a relief to doze off and leave all responsibility on his shoulders. Arriving and boarding remains a haze. The captain and the other crew member appear out of the darkness and there is an intense period of activity as we board and the two crewmen get suited up in oilskins and boots. As a guest, not wanting to be in the way, get soaked, or fall overboard, I stay in the cabin with the captain.

As the boat motors out the channel to the open water in the early dawn, I see we are not alone. Several other boats are ahead and behind us. "It's an average day for wave height and wind," they tell me. I find myself in the cabin, standing along the centre of the boat clinging to a chrome support pipe that holds up the dining table. If I sit at the inner end of the table (toward the outside of the boat), my bottom refuses to stay attached to the bench as the boat pitches. Flying up an inch or two is OK, but re-connecting with the bench is *most uncomfortable.* I am unsure of deck activities. It may be cowardly to stay in the cabin, but at least they won't have to stop fishing to look for me when I am inevitably pitched over the side by a big wave. In addition, it is much warmer inside. My biggest fear is to embarrass myself by getting seasick but, praise the Lord, there is no sign of any uneasiness.

I have brought a camera to take photographs to use in my photo business, but I realize I forgot to load high-speed film.

Between the darkness and the motion of the boat, the early shots will prove to be useless. My favourite picture of the entire trip (on the next page) is taken of the sunrise out over the water with perhaps 20 fishing boats all in the same general area. It looks like some sort of marine picnic on the water!

The captain uses his GPS and chart display system to get to the first set of traps. Fishing, especially earlier in the season, is a very exhausting activity. In May it is often bitterly cold—especially with the damp winds over the water—and the waves make the deck quite unstable. The two crew members are wearing waterproofs—trousers, coat, and boots—to try to stay dry and warm. In the early light before sunrise the boat reaches the first lobster traps and they begin pulling them up. A hydraulic winch pulls up

Sunrise Among the Lobster Boats

the string of traps. Six traps are roped together in a string with perhaps 10 feet of line between each trap. Longer ropes at each end of the string lead to personalized marker floats—a unique colour combination for each fisherman. A lobster license allows 300 traps, so that means we have 50 strings to locate and pull today. After a string of 6 traps comes up on deck (usually somehow lined up along a rail or a centre platform), the crew opens the tops and empties out any lobsters, and re-baits the traps as necessary. They work flat out much of the time. These days, most lobster traps are square with plastic-coated netting between the frame pieces. A few traps of the classic arched wooden shape still exist, but these are now sold to tourists who tie them to the roof of their cars and haul them home to give a nautical look to their yards. Back on the boat, once the traps are emptied, unless the captain has decided to relocate the string elsewhere in hopes of a better catch, at his signal the first trap gets a push over the edge. As that trap sinks, the interconnecting rope pulls each trap in turn over the edge into the water as the boat moves along. I'm told it is possible, if someone is careless, to be caught in the rope as it pays out and be pulled overboard.

The crew keeps busy sorting lobsters for size and sex. Don't ask me how to sex a lobster, but the small ones and the pregnant females are tossed back into the ocean while rubber bands go over the claws of the keepers. These last lobsters are sorted as either *canners* or the larger *markets*. There are also *jumbos,* but these are rare.

The captain meanwhile is steering the boat to the next string. GPS coordinates were saved for each string as it was dropped yesterday so the boat need only return to those same coordinates to locate its distinctly-coloured floats. A float on each ends gives redundancy—if you lose one float, you can still find the string by the float on the other end. All strings are, by local agreement, laid in the same direction (east-west in this case). Since other fishermen's strings may be set as close as 20 feet away, to put them out crosswise would be to invite a horrible tangle. I am told that is not just a hypothetical problem.

Summoning my courage, I go out on the deck to get a few pictures of lobsters, but everything out there is wet, slippery, and open to the sea. It never does get *warm* on the water that day even though it is late June—near the end of the season. We dock a little after noon with something like 500 pounds of orange/grey lobster in plastic tanks on the deck.

Having experienced the life of a fisherman (albeit briefly) I will never again dare to even imagine that lobster fishing is an easy job!

Early Crossing On The Ferry

This article describes the sights and sounds of an early-morning trip going from Wood Islands, P.E.I. to Caribou, Nova Scotia on the Confederation—the larger of the two ferryboats in service there.

Why do so many of my ferry trips start in the dark? Here my wife and I sit in our car, about seventh in line, still half-asleep, waiting for an orange-coated worker to direct us onto the boat. It is just barely summer. Faint signs of dawn are visible to the left, but the car is a warm, safe haven from the strange, dark surroundings. Ahead of us, a few older men travelling by themselves are whiling away the time standing by their pickups discussing whatever they discuss. To the right is a long line of waiting semi-trucks—most of them look to be carrying pulp logs for the paper mill or going to fetch Nova Scotia gravel. It is our first time crossing and I hesitate to venture far from the car—perhaps they will *suddenly* require us to start the car and board the ferry, and I would cause a delay, and everyone would be angry with me! After the rush to get here early enough, afraid of missing the ferry or finding it too full, we are safely in line. No hurdle remains but to try to relax after the initial shock of getting up so early.

Later runs are more scenic, but we have a medical appointment in Halifax and hope to be home before dark. In the back of our minds lurk vague horror stories of missing a crossing because

Confederation Ferry at Dock

the ferry fills up before you get on.

All at once, the total lethargy is gone. The staff person has driven her little golf cart to the front of *our* line, and now the first car is moving. On up the ramp we go, a tiny train of traffic going up the ramp and disappearing down into the big boat. There is a moment of buzzing as the tires go over the metal mesh gangplank (if it was later and you were awake, you could look down and see through the mesh openings to the water far below). The line of cars drops down a steep ramp into the bowels (that's the only word that fits!) of the ship.

Everything down here is bright with artificial lights reflecting off glossy-painted steel walls and ceiling. Each blindly following the car ahead, our tiny train of cars moves toward the front of the ferry. "Park right here," signals the attendant. Instantly all the knowledgeable people around us are climbing out of their vehicles, gathering jackets and other possessions, and heading for the outside stairways. Looking toward the completely empty back of the deck, we realize many more cars could easily have fit—there was never any danger of being excluded from this trip! (We now know that overflow is almost unknown except in mid-summer and then only on runs around the middle of the day as tourists move to the next phase of their vacation. For tourists without a pressing schedule, missing a ferry run actually becomes an opportunity to saunter out onto the wharf for a close up look at the fishing boats, or to amble over to the lighthouse and look out on the Strait).

Trudging up the stairs (there are elevators for those who take the time to find them), we go up three levels to the deck. Our choice of the nearest stairway brings us out on one side of the open deck rather than inside the passenger area. Sitting out on deck in this chilly pre-dawn hour is out of the question! A short walk takes us across to the cafeteria. Here everything is light, warm, and bustling. First arrivals are lining up for breakfast. Having stuffed down a little food before we left home, we go forward and on up to the next level. Here we find rows and rows of vinyl-padded seats firmly anchored to the floor. At one end a TV is blaring out the morning news, so we continue our wandering to the relatively quiet other end. There is not a soul in the room, so we go from place to place trying to decide which seats are the best. The ventilators seem to make a draft by *these* seats. *Those* seats are too close to the outer door and may get cold air in. *That* end has a TV and may be noisy if someone turns it on. Finally we settle. My wife has come equipped with a collection of puzzle books and sets to work. To me everything is much too exciting for sitting or reading—I go out on the forward deck to look around.

To the left (the *port* side for any mariners in the audience) it is getting lighter, and I can begin to make out the small shacks and boats in the fishing harbour, the lighthouse with its occasional flash, and far off to the east, the pink tint of early dawn. Walking around to the centre of the forward deck, I see the channel we will take out through 'the steels' to Northumberland Strait. It looks like today will be calm. Far out on the water, I can just see lights of what must be a fishing boat already pulling lobster traps. Far, far across, just above the grey of the water, is the darker blue of the Nova Scotia hills where we are heading. Walking around to the right (the *starboard* side), I see the marsh area inside the harbour limits with a few herons already working the shallows. A confused, raucous, swirl of gulls marks where the water is churned up just in front of the ferry. The propulsion system is kept idling just enough to keep the boat pressed against the dock. While we were getting settled, the interior loading ramp was raised and the semi-trucks have gone aboard the upper vehicle deck. They will be the first ones off on the other end.

Suddenly a short blast of the ferry's whistle, announces it is about to depart. 'Blast' is the only suitable word for such a loud noise that close! I suspect some ferry captains derive a malicious pleasure from seeing how high their unsuspecting passengers jump! The rumble under foot changes and, leaning over to look down at the narrow space between the ferry and the tires cushioning the sides of the ferry slip, I see we have started to creep forward. I hurry back across to the east side and watch the fishing shacks begin to drop behind.

Our rate of movement increases. I look across at the lighthouse and realize that sometime in there dawn changed to sunrise. The few thin clouds in the east mean it is going to be a grey and

Wood Islands Light at Sunrise

pink sunrise—none of the drama a photographer would desire. How many other people in the area are appreciating this very same quiet sunrise? Still picking up speed, we pass through the outer channel (between 'the steels') and reach the open water. To the east is a perfect photo op—red, sandy shore leading toward the Wood Islands lighthouse, a few mild waves breaking and, on the horizon, a far point of land extending out behind the lighthouse cliff, all crowned by the pink sunrise. Now the sun appears around a few low clouds and the day has begun.

As land drops rapidly back, our speed creates a wind. It is unexpectedly chilly for a summer day and I'm wearing only a light sweatshirt. Wrestling open the heavy door, I slip into the warmth and light of the sitting area. My wife continues working in her puzzle book. Perhaps I will sit in here with her and wait out the rest of the 75-minute crossing. No, a few minutes later, I pop up and casually go outside to make sure I'm not missing something. There is not much to see in the middle of the Strait—no ships, no sailboats, no marine life. On a calm day such as this, there is barely even a discernible roll to the boat—it promises to be a dull crossing. (If you should happen to take any of the mid-day, in-season crossings, I have been told there is much more activity, including live entertainment and, of course, many more passengers. If you cross in an Autumn storm, I'm told there can be excitement of a different sort, but the runs are cancelled if the wind or waves are too high).

Eventually, our ferry approaches the far shore. A small lighthouse appears on the Nova Scotia shore far to our right, and soon we are moving between the red and green channel buoys. Close to the left side our channel takes us by a sandy point of land. Now I can see a fishing harbour ahead to the left and the ferry docks straight in front. There is the other ferry, the *Holiday Island*, tied up waiting for the busy season. Just when all sorts of interesting activity is picking up, the loud speakers announce (from later experience, far too early to be taken seriously), "Time to go to your vehicles." A sudden unease sets in, "What if we procrastinate and they are ready to unload before we have gotten to the car?" Down we hurry the 3 or 4 levels to the passenger-car deck and squeeze over to our car. Safely inside, we sit there interminably, feeling safe but closed in. There is a slight vibration through the tires from the deck, but the noise level has dropped.

Eventually the ferry connects to the dock and big trucks on the upper level go ashore. The inside ramp comes down and the attendant directs our small line of cars off the boat. Up the steep ramp, across the open-grid gangway to shore, and off we zoom like a swarm of angry hornets. We cross an open area where cars have lined up for the return trip and then our road narrows in to 2-lanes. Vehicles jockey for position as though it is a road race. By the time we have negotiated the rotary and the causeway across to the paper mill, traffic has thinned out and we become ordinary travellers heading for Halifax.

Where Has My Boat Gone?

Over the past few years I have developed a significant problem. It began the first year I launched my sailboat and crops up on an annoyingly regular basis every year. I call it the *Lost Boat Syndrome*. It is a particularly annoying malady because I do everything in my power to effect a cure, and still it pops up every year. It is similar to Anne in *Anne of Green Gables* explaining that she never makes the same mistake twice—unfortunately she keeps finding *new* mistakes to make. In much the same way, I keep finding new ways to lose my boat from its mooring or anchorage. Let me give you a few instances:

1) The first year the boat was in the Wood Islands harbour I got a knock on the door one rainy, windy night. It was a neighbour reporting that my boat was on the sandbar on the eastern side of the harbour. He was graciously met me there and, sure enough, the boat showed up in the headlights getting washed against the sandbar with the prospect of the increasing tide bringing it to pound

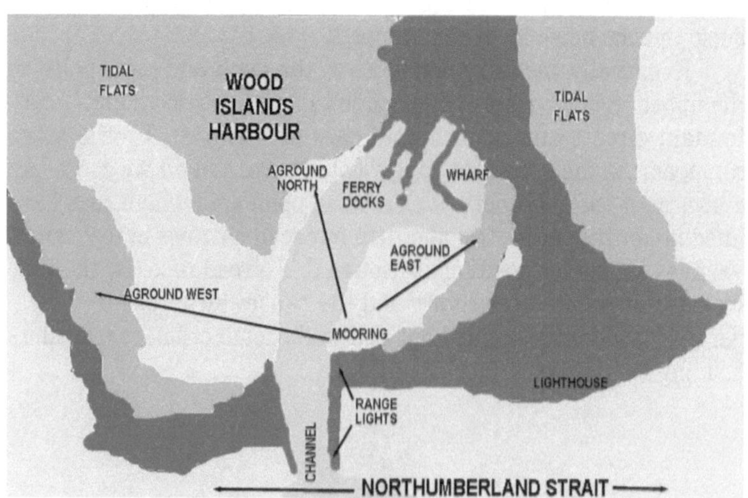

*Map of Wood Islands Harbour
Showing Boat Wanderings*

against the concrete blocks placed to prevent erosion. About then my friend's boat came bobbing along, having also shed its mooring connection. Between two fishermen and my friend we rowed a line to each boat in succession and were able to drag them across to the sheltered harbour with a pickup truck. There they were firmly tied for the night. Subsequent investigation indicated that my friend's boat had chafed through the mooring rope while mine had broken a ring that held the float and chain to the boat's line.

2) Later that year, with a chafe guard around the mooring line, the line separated *under* the guard and the boat blew over to the West side of the harbour.

3) The next year I sailed with a friend to Murray Harbour and left the boat anchored overnight. Coming back the next day, there was no sign of it! Scanning the water, I finally saw it about a mile away, almost going out into the open water. Three young people went out in my small dinghy to rescue it and had no end of trouble getting to it and bringing it back. We tied it to a vacant mooring and concluded that the anchor had not been let out far enough to hold in the high tides—in nautical terms, there was not enough *scope*.

4) The next year I got a 6:30 am call from the ferry: would I please move my boat as it is sitting in the channel and blocking departure of the ferry? Sure enough, while it had moved enough to be out of the way, it was not attached to its mooring and was almost

Ferry Leaving Harbour

hitting the second ferry. A rescue in the dinghy had all sorts of problems, but the basic cause was the opening of a shackle that held the chain to the concrete mooring block. A tiny wire holds the pin from rotating, but apparently a non-stainless one had rusted through and the pin had come unscrewed, leaving the boat attached to a chain with nothing on the end.

Early Morning at Machon's Point

5) This last year we sailed again to Murray Harbour (Machon's Point) and left the boat tied to a vacant mooring—no more anchoring for us! The next day I get a call from a resident living nearby that my boat is on their beach. Sure enough, getting there at dusk I discovered it leaning sharply to one side because the keel is on the ground and the tide has gone back out. Consulting the tide charts, I find that I can float it off at 2 am, so I come back and return it to the mooring. The flaw had been that I relied on a pickup rope off the mooring, and a knot in the end came untied. With a chain around the heavy rope *under* the float, there was no further trouble.

6) You would think that would be enough for one year. Unfortunately on Thanksgiving Day I found a message on my answering

machine asking if my "punt" was over at "MacLean's Beach" (which we guessed was on the West side of the harbour).

"Impossible," I thought, "It is sitting on the sailboat in the yard."

A quick trip out to the sailboat and, "OOPS, it is not on the boat."

We made a hurried drive down to the harbour and looked out. On the western sandbar was a tiny object that might be the dinghy. There was a strong wind out of the West and it looked as though the rising tide might wash it off and send it back across the harbour. We hurried home and drove back to the start of the sand spit. My wife kept watch from the truck as I strode out toward what might be my dinghy, the oars over my shoulder and a heavy sweatshirt to fight off the wind chill. We agreed that, if I was able to launch the dinghy and began rowing across, she would drive around and meet me on the shore near the lighthouse.

It was a long hike to the boat—the sand made walking very tiring, and a sense of urgency added speed to my steps. As I got nearer, it seemed that the object might well be my dark-green dinghy. It is about 6' long and made out of plywood and epoxy (called "stitch & glue" construction). The nearer I got, the more I imagined it was rocking in the wind and likely to go afloat before I got there. When I actually arrived, it was clear that 1) it was actually my dinghy; 2) it was solidly buried in the sand and full of water. I could not even budge it until I used an oar to splash out the water. Beneath the layer of water was about 6" of sand, but once the water was out, I was able to tip the dinghy over and empty out the sand. I dragged it 20' or so to the water and was about to launch when I realised the flotation chambers were waterlogged. Despite a life jacket, I took time to drain the chambers—I may have been careless about tying up the boat but I was not stupid. The strong southwest wind was almost behind me, so rowing was relatively easy. In order to reach a place where it would be easy to put it in the truck, I had to row crosswise to the wind for a while. Then it was straight downwind to my landing place. The tiny boat bobbed along with no problem. The waves had not gone far enough into the harbour to grow very large. Rowing in big waves can be fun if you are not at risk of being blown out to sea. Unlike a large boat, a tiny dinghy easily bobs up over the waves and would only be at risk if a big wave broke just as it was passing. As I neared the landing, I saw the truck zipping around to meet me. Loaded into the truck, my little boat was soon home where it belonged.

How could I miss a dinghy for about 10 days? I am sure it was tied to the sailboat when the latter was pulled out for the winter. Having the mast break and then losing the trailer bearings on the way home must have driven it out of mind. I was quite sure it was tied on the deck until that call came many days later. The poor dinghy must have wandered around the harbour for about 2 weeks, driven by the winds and tide until it finally ran aground at a high tide and got locked in the sand. It is amazing to think how well it stood up to all that pounding after it was locked in.

As I look back on the 5 years or so, it seems like a comedy of errors. I am resolved to conquer in the end (whenever that is). But on top of all that, I am amazed at the helpfulness of the various people who have watched over my wandering boats. What they must think of me, I have no idea, but their patience is impressive. I hope I am as willing to help when someone else is in need.

Leslie Stewart

My name is Leslie Stewart. My wife Dorrie and I live in a big old yellow farmhouse with sunflowers painted on one side of our home, in Sturgeon P.E.I.

We used to live in Cambridge, then one day, the Roads Department moved the sign, and now we are fish people living in Sturgeon.

I began writing poems in 2007. My first poem was about our neighbour, who would come over and blow out our driveway after a winter storm. I now write about the whole Island, and lands far beyond.

I hope you enjoy what you read. I enjoyed writing them.

A Lobster's Tale

Oh, I say, "A tug, a heave and a ho,
Up from the bottom I did go".
Oh, I say, "A tug, a heave and a ho.
Let this poor lobster go."

Why I was just out there just crawling by,
when food in a wood trap caught my eye.
There was a tug, a heave and a ho.
Up from the bottom, I did go.
The ugly mug said "Hey, look what I got—
another fine lobster for our boiling pot"
So I said "Hey, life at the bottom is better for me.
So you ugly mug, throw me back in the sea!"

He never knew we could converse this way.
I fell out of his hands and crawled away.
He tried to grab me as I fell,
But all he got was a lobster's tale.
I headed back down to the bottom of the sea.
That had been too much of an adventure for me.
Now the ugly mug dove in, chasing me down.
I thought for sure that he might drown.

Oh, I say, "A tug, a heave and a ho.
Up from the bottom he did go".
Oh, I say, "A tug, a heave and a ho.
Let that poor lobster fisherman go."

Now this was more like home, and better for me,
way out there on the bottom of the sea.
If you're ever fishing out in Boughton Island Bay,
they tell the story of the talking lobster that got away.

I still say, "A tug, a heave and a ho.
Let this poor lobster go."
Oh I say "A tug, a heave and a ho.
Let this poor lobster go."

Bicycle Memories

An old bicycle, my father gave to me,
*   old and rusted by the sea.*
It was everything you see—
*   my father gave it, just to me.*
"Ride that bike," he said to me.
*   "Off you go, there's an Island to see."*
Ride this bike for old memories.
*   I couldn't ride that bike my father gave to me.*
The handlebars had rusted away.
*   With twine and a stick, we fixed it to stay.*
The tires, they were flat, they had no air.
*   We filled them with lots of old horsehair.*
I said "Father, there is no seat."
*   He said, "Don't despair,*
*   son. Look over there.*
You can use that old outhouse seat.
*   There's lots of old memories on there."*
I was short, the bike it was tall,
*   but that didn't bother me at all.*
When I began to pedal, the tires didn't spin.
*   My father stood there with a wide grin.*
The chain had rusted. It was gone,
*   but there lay another on the lawn.*
When we added wire and twine,
*   the chain, it worked just fine.*
Finally I was ready, the Island to see.
*   This bike was a magic carpet to me.*
*   This old bicycle my father gave to me.*
Yes, it's full of old memories.
*   Yes, it's full of old memories.*

Bottle Man

Bottle Man, Bottle Man, who can be that bottle Man?

Rides his bike, most every day,
picking up bottles gone astray.
Most folks lose them from their car
Open windows, they can throw them far.

Bottle Man, Bottle Man, who can be that bottle Man?

It's a good thing he has a bike,
way too far for the old guy to hike.
Wears a helmet and a safety vest, too.
This old guy cleans up for me and you.

Bottle Man, Bottle Man, who can be that bottle Man?

I've seen him working in early morn.
Then once we saw him in a thunderstorm.
Lightning didn't hit him, he was doing alright.
Did you ever see the bottle-picker's bike?

Bottle Man, Bottle Man, who can be that bottle Man?

Picking up pop bottles, beer ones too.
Can it be Bud, Canadian or Blue.
Short stubby bottles, they got no neck
Tall or stubby with no neck.
He picks them up, saying, "What the heck."

Bottle Man, Bottle Man, who can be that bottle Man?

If you're ever over Montague way,
You just might see him working that day.
Loads his bike, to the Depot he goes,
Recycles those bottles for a million or so.

Bottle Man, Bottle Man, who can be that bottle Man?

People drive by, their kids will say
He picks up bottles gone astray.
There may not be much time for him.
Those bottles soon may turn to tin.

Bottle Man, Bottle Man, who can be that bottle Man?

Gaspereaux

There once was a man from Gaspereaux who had a dog,
and together they would go
Off to sea for lobster and fish.
That faithful dog, he ate from his dish.
Into the bush they would go for firewood and lumber.
That dog, he pulled those heavy logs
and yet he never slumbered.

Oh how that dog did swear
The man from Gaspereaux and his dog did go.
Many a time to town, they would go,
Master in the cab with air, heat and radio—
the dog in the back, Walking around,
bugs in his teeth, dirt on his frown
The dog had heat on hot summer days.
Didn't have a hat to keep off the rays

Oh how that dog did swear
The man from Gaspereaux and his dog did go.
The dog had air on cold winter days
Eyes watering, throat sore, he had air.
No scarf, no toque, no mittens to wear.
Master in the cab with heat, radio to play.
People would look, and people would say
He loves his dog. His dog loves it that way.

Oh how that dog did swear.
The man from Gaspereaux and his dog did go.
When the time comes, and it did one day,
The Master he did finally pass away.
The dog visits the Master in the ground.
As he sits nearby, with that dog-like frown
remembering his trips to town
Oh how that dog did swear,
the man from Gaspereaux and his dog did go.

Good Times or Hard Times

I'm dreaming of my family and Island home. They're all I have and love, so far away. I'm working in the oil fields out in Albert— digging on this cold, God-awful November day.

Only to be digging for clams, or fishing at sea, or walking with my wife, holding her hand. Instead, I'm breaking this frozen ground with pick and hammer, working the land.

They said this was to be the promised land; the West was the place I should be. Money flowed and jobs, they were plenty. They said "It was like kelp from the sea."

Now I live with my good buddy and five hundred more like me. We came searching for our future. That is back home, fishing in the sea. No jobs on the Island for men like us.

Where are farmers, fishermen, and carpenters by trade? Times are sorry poor. No money, and debts to the sky. We left wives, children, parents and friends we made.

The small towns are getting even smaller. Some villages are gone. No one seems to care. Country roads and lanes aren't travelled anymore. Cars sit empty, tractors rest in lonely fields of despair.

I'll take a rest and sit on this frozen old stump. The forests here have much in common with the sea. They change colour, and rise and fall forever. Snow rests on their tops, as breaking waves would be.

So, it's back to work, and swing that heavy hammer. I'm breaking up the ground, another road to repair. Tom from Kinross yells to Robert from Murray River "Did you see that dog last night?" "That's no dog – it's a bear." Now, that sent a chill from my backside to my head.

Never saw a bear before, but I've seen a whale or two. Funny how my mind works. It always takes me back home. It hurts me now inside, because I'm thinking of you.

We have music here at the camp. Some men do the jig, one guy plays the spoons, and fiddlers, we have a few. Two old guys play the banjo, another dozen can sing.

This old guy from Cambridge, he tells a joke or two.

Most of us have travelled by boat, truck or rail, just to get here to Alberta, before the heavy snow. There will be no homesick here, for here you have to stay. When Spring is around the corner, then home we will go.

I see the Rocky Mountains, way off in the distance, dark grey and blue, with ragged tops and round. They remind me of a summer storm on the Island. Clouds rise and bank together, then the rain comes down.

The days are getting longer, the sun is warming up. I'll be able to sleep in my long johns soon. I wear my parka all day, and heavy blankets at night. I am a little nervous with five hundred men in a room.

Old Walter Dixon heard a train the other day. He said, "The whistle sounded like the ferry at Woods Island calling us to be ready to board, soon time to go home." We all laughed and smiled to the very last man.

The road was finally done, and there was the corner. Spring had come at last, time to head back East. Some men had already left. Others waited for their last pay. I was glad to be heading home, just to say the least.

As we travelled back home by rail, the ship of the land, we Islanders became young children at play. It was much like waiting at Christmas, under the tree. Time to open our presents, and we'll be home to stay.

The roads are still dusty, times are still sorry poor. We brought home some hope, and we pay the bills. My tractor ploughs a field to plant some potatoes. We all hope that hard times are over, and say it's God's will.

I made new friends while working out West. Some live around the corner, others far away. My wife is going to have another baby, so it's good times or hard times—home I'll stay.

I Lost My Boat on St. Mary's Bay

I lost my boat on St. Mary's Bay.
The sad site still haunts me today.
She was my dream, hand-built by me,
Crafted over the winter. I worked endlessly.

Cutting, gluing, sanding with care.
Finger joints, dovetails, lots of hardware.
Brass screws, stainless and four-inch nails,
I had her name on my mind, I knew it well.

I was an Island boy, but now a man.
No need for those blueprint plans.
I've known that Bay all my time,
watched the tides cine and go. I'll be fine.

I've worked on mussel boats,
Lobster boats, anything that floats.
Spring was coming on fast.
I knew winter wouldn't last.

The ice was melting on the Bay.
Yes, soon it would be my day.
I'm not a dreamer, I'm a man.
I've built that boat the best I can.

Got some special paint for dories.
Mine was bigger than that, sorry.
This was a real ship, a Man of War,
Built for adventure, high seas and more.

I painted her sunset orange and red.
"Sharp-looking craft," my friend said.
It was now mid-April. The ice melted away.
Yes, very soon, it would be my day.

The name was hand-painted by me.
She was now ready for the sea.
Life jacket? Not for this seaman.
I will not bob in the water—swim I can.

Onto the Bay. The water was ice-blue.
The water's a little cold. It will do
Off I go, as many a sailor before me,
With a mighty stroke, set off to sea.

A little water started to come in.
Maybe the glue had been a little too thin.
I ave it no real need for worry.
This was my day. I was in a hurry.

Now the dory paint is looking really good.
Maybe I shouldn't have used some new wood.
The outhouse walls—they'll float, you know.
I had asked the Home Lumber guy. He said so.

Finally, I was out there on St. Mary's Bay.
A lot of water was coming in the boat, not OK.
The water lapped over the gunnels.
I had forgotten the bucket, I couldn't bail.

It was soon time to abandon ship.
Springing overboard, I slipped a disk.
I saw my dream ship sink that day.
If I only had a life jacket, to bob in the Bay.

The stern rose out of St. Mary's Bay.
There with her proud name on display.
I knew it was a gesture of good-bye.
And that brought tears to my eyes.

She was a good ship. I called her the EI
There will never be another like her, bye.
Employment Insurance had built that ship for me.
It had funded my ship that sank in the sea.

I lost my ship on St. Mary's Bay.
I hope when your ship comes in today
You will spend your fortune a different way
Than to have your ship sink in St. Mary's Bay.

I'm Coming Back Home to P.E.I.

I'm coming back home to P.E.I.
Coming back home to P.E.I.
There are tears in my eyes
I'm coming back home to P.E.I.

I've been to places you have never seen.
It wasn't very nice there, they hated me.
That's why I'm coming back home to P.E.I.
Ho, I'm coming back home to P.E.I.

I saw people dying, starvation everywhere
It's no place to be for an Island boy like me.
They say "Go back to the land that is free."
Ho, I'm coming back home to P.E.I.
Coming back home to P.E.I.

This is my sad story, for you to tell.
I served my country, did my job in Hell
They gave me the flag and a star as well.
I'm coming back home to P.E.I.
Coming back home to P.E.I.

They will bury me, everyone will cry,
There was no reason for me to die.
Bury me in that red clay of hope
I'm back home, home on P.E.I.
Back home, home on P.E.I.

You say "Goodbye" with tears in your eyes.
I'm back home, home in P.E.I.

Our Island Home

It was on the Internet we bought this Island home. In the pictures, it stood there on a hill, all alone. You could tell it had been a proud old farmhouse, and now it was waiting there, just for us.

The first time I saw the real estate ad, this poor looking, rundown farmhouse was sad. There was no happiness left in the poor old place. It sure was looking sad, as if it had lost the race.

Now I was at home, searching the web that night. I had been looking for a cheap house, alright. Called the realtor, say his name is Barry.

"No problem," he said, "You can take the bridge or the ferry."

"That's OK," I said, "but you see, I'm too far away."

"It's a good deal," he replied. "Better not delay."

I said I was interested, and would let him know. "Oh, by the way, you get very much snow?"

In the picture, you see, there was snow on the ground. It covered everything—only the sad house I found. Not a shed or a barn, not even a garage for the car. So, move to Prince Edward Island— that is pretty far.

In a few days, I called Barry back to say, "We'll buy that house, and move there to stay."

In a puzzled voice, he said, "You'll be from away?"

"No," said I. "If we move there, we won't be from away, eh?"

The time had come at last—Moving Day. All our things packed or jammed in OK. It's a long two-day trip, driving a moving van, leaving Ontario, going to our new promised land.

This was to be our first visit to our new home. The deal was done. We were here at last, home alone. After walking around the house, going very slow, my first thought was—get back in the truck and go.

Maybe I should light a match, if I had one. Cremate the old house. I felt a coward—I wanted to run. My heart sank deep, those first precious minutes or so. Had I bitten off way too much? This I didn't know.

The house hadn't seen paint, maybe since Confederation. There was a couple of fridges over some plywood creation. It seemed to be a basement entrance from outside. I had a thought, opened the door to one. No beer inside.

The back porch or shed or call it what you may, they tell me now, it was a kitchen in its day. But today it's full of junk, and holes in its floor. I carried the first of our belongings through the door.

On the way out, I see a wasp nest on the wall. Now today, that didn't bother me at all. Each time I went from the truck to the house, my thoughts were—This isn't fit for an Island mouse.

Better see how to turn on the water, in case I have to pee. Went down to the basement—none of it made sense to me. By now, my back was hurting—it was starting to ache. This was as good a time as any to take my first Island break.

I walked over to my brand new neighbours to say, "Hi." As it turns out, well, he's a hell of a nice guy. In fact, it was he who shut off the water, you see. He would be glad to turn it back on, but first, biscuits and tea.

I liked the hospitality. It made me feel alright. But that didn't help me sleep my first night. There was more work to be done than I first thought. Lots of windows, floors and doors had dry rot.

The basement wall on one side was falling down. This was my first job. Cement and gravel I found. So I poured a new wall of concrete to hold up this one. My hard work wasn't over. Hell, it hadn't begun.

On sunny days, we scraped, we painted, and worked on our tans. On rainy days, we knocked down walls. Imagine if you can, tearing out plaster. The house was thick in dust as fog. My wife made me work so hard, at night I slept like a log.

Neighbours and just friendly folks dropped by to say hello. They would all agree—that's a lot of work, don't you know. I am quite proud to say we did some hard work really fast. We started in June and by July the outside was done at last. Friends and family from Ontario, far away, came down to see us and spent some summer days as people who came to the Island to make it their home. We took our friends and family. The Island we roamed.

It was just after Old Home Week, I remember so well. I had this dream. Paint flowers on a wall, that don't smell. Sunflowers it was to be. Not one or two, but three. They would be twelve feet high, ten wide, painted by me.

We soon became known as *the sunflower guys*. We also had real sunflowers, some nine feet high. There's purple ones, cream yellow, regular type, multiple heads. Sunflowers turn their heads from morning till time for bed.

With all this work done to the old farmhouse, she looks OK. She has a new colour, fresh smile, she was alive, they say. We gave her new glass. No cracks, no broken panes.

She looks good now, happy, friendly—and we felt the same. We lived in Cambridge Ontario, for quite a spell. Then we moved down to Cambridge, P.E.I. Oh well. One day I woke up, and noticed they had moved the sign.

So now, we live in Sturgeon P.E.I. Heck, we don't mind. Now the next year, I painted more flowers to the wall—a couple of butterflies, one great big, the other small.

We're still working on the property. Built a workshop for me, my wife got a carport, a side porch. It's not the same, you see.

On the Island, folks say, a happy house is never alone. So Give it a call, use your phone. Now two cats live here, it's their house as well. And they're very happy, that you can tell.

As we drive about the Island on Discovery Days, many houses we see have been left the same way. These are proud houses, not fair to be left to decay. So come and add life to a home, you people from away.

the Sunflower House

Rusty M. Nails

This a true story.
Well, more of a rumor, you know,
About an old fellow named Nails.
Made moonshine in his house, the story goes,

Over the years of trying, you will learn how,
So it took Nails a long time just to get it right.
Years went by, but he could brew OK now.
The hard part is not getting caught, as you might.

People would talk a lot about where to get some brew,
And as these folks talked, the Mounties were listening.
So over a long time, the Mounties thought they knew
That Nails was doing more than fishing and whistling.

Folks around Souris, North Cape and Little Pond
Were well-maintained in good homemade brew.
It seems that Mister Nails and the Law, they got on,
Because when the Law came, it seems that Nails knew.

Now in order to be a successful business man,
You should always have goals to reach.
Our moonshiner had a dandy plan;
Not only did he talk to people, he would preach.

"Don't be drinking alcohol—It's the Devil's way".
Nails often told folks that, when a Mountie was in sight.
"If you start drinking, Satan will be at your door someday."
That was his way of telling folks, "New brew ready tonight."

He had another way of throwing the law off his trail.
Nails is a coffin or casket maker, sort of a sideline.
When you went to his old house, only varnish did you smell.
He always had a brush or two dipped in a jar of bad turpentine.

It seems that when the Law would pay a visit by surprise,
They only found Nail adding another coat of clear.
You see, Nail lived outside of town, just on a rise.
He had the only house on the lane, no others were near.

You could look out the shed window and see the town.
This as a good location, for the final touches of the brew.
You could also see the Mounties if they were around.
Now most folks in town let on that they never knew.

Our boy, Mister Nails, never sold a casket or coffin.
The stench of the old varnish covered the smell.
You see, he revarnished that same one quite often.
The basement was full of shine, but you couldn't tell.

So remember what I said, true story or not.
The only one who knows is buried well below,
In a well-varnished casket that will never rot.
But ask the folks from Souris, they might know.

So here we have it—the moral to a sad story.
It's one we hear most often.
When you start drinking, you'd better worry.
Are you adding another Nail to a coffin?

Georgetown Ceilidh

When you come to the Georgetown Ceilidhs, you know
The ladies here well, they run the whole show
They invite you in, say hello and take your money
Yes, these ladies are as busy as bees to honey
They dance the floor, serve the food and play the spoons
Wish you a happy birthday now and if it's coming soon
You will get a birthday cake with candles a burning bright
Yes, Georgetown is the place to come to party alright

Georgetown Ceilidhs are a lot of fun
It's a place so special to everyone
Lots of people singing and dancing every night
Those great performers put on a show alright
You can't sit down, no longer than a song?
A friendly person says hay come along
You can't be sitting while there's a dance floor
That what folks come all the way here for

It's the partings place on a Tues. night
Everyone upbeat, no one's uptight
The ceilidh food is the best for miles around
Another good reason to come to Georgetown
They all dress up for special occasions too
Wear that crazy hat, no one laughs at you
I asked when the Ceilidh's here all began
It started with two small girls drumming pop cans

Now they play the fiddle and guitar
One smokes cigarettes the other cigars
The Ceilidhs will live on long after we're gone
Our grandchildren will be singing those songs
So come to a Georgetown Ceilidh on Tues. night
Crazy dressed up people are a wonderful sight
The ladies here are running a hell of a show
I just thought that you would like to know

They welcomed me in so I could read a story or two
And I make the long dive here just to read to you
They said we can all miss a night some times
So I'll keep coming as long as the words rhyme

Island Gone South

When this story all came about, it had started up west. A group of fishermen were drinking, on a cold stormy night. The power had gone off again at the Christopher Cross Arms Hotel. Talk of spring and sunshine, lobster fishing and warm weather was in the air. Then one got to thinking, why stay on the island in the wintertime? A warmer place would be best.

A better place to be at this time would be in the Caribbean. So they hatched this plan, to relocate the island. How many would really go? Lots of folks like the snow. Some liked ice fishing and snow sledding. Bob's wife would miss skiing at Brookvale and what about hockey? A pause filled the air on that one—we can watch it on TV—not fair to take everyone all the way to the warmer sun.

It would work, that they knew but not all the people just a few. Better inform the good folks from down east of this marvellous plan, lots of people go away down there when they can. Then there came the size of island? We needed just a small island and many names they went through, until it came down to two.

Boughton Island or Pictou. Which one would be the easiest to tow?

They would spend this time to plan, and move the island when they can. They figured it would take many boats to move the island fast enough so it would stay afloat. Pictou was chosen, the island to be, spending our winter on in the warm Caribbean Sea.

Not many people lived on Pictou Island in the summer time and none in the wintertime that I know. That would all change next winter in the snow. Will it take long and how will she tow? Will the island need a bow and a stern? All these things did cause a concern.

It would be easy to steal; they thought so. The island belonged to Nova Scotia, not us they wouldn't miss it, so no big fuss.

It was decided that since the plan started up west, it would be best to have a captain from there. Names went around and one was found. It would be Robert Shaw, Captain Rob from Miminegash— he would be our man. He would lead us south when he can. Some fishermen thought a summer run of a couple of boats would do, just check out the times, distance, get a better handle on what we have to go through. Made a raft threw on some clay so they could plant some potatoes along the way.

Captain Rob could organize the size of fleet that would be needed for such a feat. A couple of hundred boats needed to do the deed. So how many people will we have to feed? How about cabins on the island to stay? If we build them now it would give our plan away. Fingers Chaisson thought, make the cabins look like lobster traps. People would never suspect, so that was that. If someone should have asked about the size of traps? We harvest big lobsters. After lobster season that year the project began. Word was spread. Let's head south for the winter when we can. Lobster trap cabins began springing up all over the island. Some were quite fancy with palm trees and vines painted on the side, while that was quite fine. Some had lobsters in swim suits, I saw one with a thong and that was all wrong.

The summer went by fast as could be; fall started and some colour was now in the trees. The day picked to leave, it was chosen last winter by a man named Gormley. He has something to do with the ferryboat and said if we had trouble moving the island the Confederation would give us hope. The thirty-first of October was moving day, if we got caught? A Halloween prank, we would say.

You wonder how this was to be done. To move an island, wouldn't be fun. They had planned the move so well it will be easy to tell. We had moved a small island in May, just pull hard and then give it a twist, just like taken the cap off a bottle beer, I wish. We did it at night so no one would see and took it for a ride. It was back by sunrise with our GPS the location was right. We did however have it turned a little from the way it used to be. The folks that used to see the land now look at the sea.

On October the 30th the fleet headed to Wood Islands. The crew of the ferry knew the plan and if we got stuck would give us a hand. At dusk ropes and anchors were pitched aground, Captain Rob gave the word, "pass it around." At 12:01, the engines let out such a roar: Pictou Island gave it a fight, but is there no more. As the sun began to rise on that October day, the fleet was well on its way.

On Guernsey Cove that day, when Gord got up to wipe the sleep from his eyes, he was in time to see Pictou island go sailing by. Before noon it was off the Cape Breton shore, other boats had joined in; now a hundred more. As the sun went down on Halloween day, we were well on our way. Just off north Sydney, they say.

The next morning some Cape Bretoners came out to ask, "What's going on?" When they heard our story, they said "Good luck" to us. We said, "If this works out as planned, next fall we'll help move your island if we can." It was agreed then by each and all Cape Breton Island in the Caribbean next fall. But first, we had this little job to get right. We hoped to get past Halifax that night.

You may wonder why so few saw this display. The fleet was traveling in a fog bank this day. Everyone had brought ice cubes from their freezers at home; when the warm Atlantic waters melted them a fog bank was formed. In the shroud of a gray fog moving along the coast, we had absconded with Pictou Island we boast.

A plan of seven days moving at this pace would put us in the Caribbean, a sunny place. If God could create the world in six days and rest, we could move an island in seven days at best. Now many stories happened along the way and these I'll write about some other day. But the point is we got there, our winter was fun and we got our E.I. check to bathe in the sun

Litter Bug

Litter Bug, Litter Bug
Go back home
Take your litter
And leave us alone

Go back to your
Province or state
Don't litter our island
For goodness sake

Leave our island
Pristine and clean
We want it the best-
Looking province you've seen

If you are an islander
Spreading litter every day
You should be ashamed of yourself
For living this way

Litter Bug, Litter Bug
Don't throw your garbage away
We love our P.E.I
Pick up your litter, today

Little Waves

The waves that are washing upon our Island shore—
have these waves been here before?
Do they know the sand of our shore?
When one comes, they always bring more.
These little waves have travelled so many miles.
Watching them play and splash, they bring a smile.
The waves wash and roll back again.
They remind us of old lost friends.
The salt, spray fills the air, with a down home smell.
"Come and play", they say. "We have stories to tell."
The little waves are so much fun for play.
That's why people come here for their holidays.
The waves laugh at Mom and Dad.
It's the most fun they have had.
The waves bring us gifts from afar.
It could be a lobster trap or a jar.
We find old driftwood washed upon the shore
from an old boat, a dock—there's always more.
The waves that are washing upon our Island shore—
have these waves been here before?
We find seaweed, stones, nets, and shells,
Mussels and sometimes an old fish that smells.
There is always lots of footprints in the sand.
The waves try to some away, if they can.
I once went away to another Island
and watched a wave washing that sand.
In the warm Caribbean, an ocean water warm.
Back home, frozen bays and snowstorms.
I asked a wave as it washed ashore,
"Have you been to Panmure Island before?"
It didn't reply and washed away.
Will I see that wave another day?

Watching the Waves